P9-CAB-108

FAMILY FRAGRANCE

*Fill Your
Home with the
Aroma of Love*

J. OTIS *&* Gail
LEDBETTER

Cook Communications

Faith Parenting is an imprint of
Cook Communications Ministries, Colorado Springs, Colorado 80918
Cook Communications, Paris, Ontario
Kingsway Communications, Eastbourne, England

FAMILY FRAGRANCE
© 1998 by J. Otis Ledbetter and Gail Hover Ledbetter.
Printed in the United States of America.

Editor: Marlee Alex
Design: Koechel Peterson and Associates
Illustrations: Chris Ellison

2 3 4 5 6 7 8 9 10 Printing/Year 02 01 00

No part of this book may be reproduced without written permission, except for brief
quotations in books and critical reviews. For information, write Chariot Victor
Publishing, 4050 Lee Vance View, Colorado Springs, Colorado 80918.

Unless otherwise noted Scripture quotations are from The New King James Version
(NKJV). © 1979, 1980, 1982, Thomas Nelson, Inc., Publishers, Nashville, Tennessee. Used
by permission. All rights reserved. Other Scripture quotations taken from the Holy
Bible: New International Version® (NIV). © 1973, 1978, 1984 by International Bible
Society. Used by permission of Zondervan Publishing House. All rights reserved. King
James Version of the Bible (KJV).

Ledbetter, J. Otis
    Family fragrance / by J. Otis Ledbetter and Gail Hover Ledbetter.
        p. cm.
    ISBN 0-78143-375-4
    1. Family—Religious life. I. Ledbetter, Gail Hover. II. Title.
    BV4526.2.L36 1998   98-4469
    248.4—dc21   CIP

Dedication

To our children
Matthew,
Rebecca and
Leah.

No classroom has taught us more about God
and His love toward us than your lives.

What we have passed to you,
may you commit to those who come behind you.

May you enjoy, and take as much pleasure in the passing
of the family legacy fragrance as we have
in passing it on to you!

This book was created as an outreach of the Heritage Builders™Association—a network of families and churches committed to passing a strong heritage to the next generation. Designed to motivate and assist families as they become intentional about the heritage-passing process, these resources draw upon the collective wisdom of parents, grandparents, church leaders, and family life experts, in an effort to provide balanced, biblical parenting advice along with effective, practical tools for family living.

For more information, write, phone, or visit our Web site:
Heritage Builders™ Association
c/o Chariot Victor Publishing   1-800-528-9489
4050 Lee Vance View   www.faithparenting.com
Colorado Springs, CO 80918   www.heritagebuilders.com

The Heritage Builders™ resources include:

Your Heritage: A foundational book explaining the Heritage Builders™ ministry's key concepts. (Trade paper)

Family Night Tool Chest books

An Introduction to Family Nights	*Basic Christian Beliefs*
Bible Stories for Preschoolers, OT	*Bible Stories for Preschoolers, NT*
Christian Character Qualities	*Holiday Family Nights*
Money Matters Family Nights	*Proverbs Family Nights*
Simple Science Family Nights	*Ten Commandments Family Nights*
Wisdom Life Skills	*Ready for Adolescence (Sept. 2000)*

Family Fragrance: Filled with ways to develop and create an AROMA of love in your home. (Trade paper)

Extending Your Heritage: Shows how the Heritage Builders™ concepts can be used by extended family and other concerned adults to pass on a spiritual legacy to children. (Trade paper)

Family Traditions: Filled with ways to celebrate old traditions and mark spiritual milestones in your family. (Trade paper)

The Family Compass: Practical help for parents as you point your child's spiritual compass toward God. (Trade paper)

Heritage Builders™ Curriculum: A small group adult study focusing on the importance of establishing and passing on a family spiritual heritage. (Thirteen-week curriculum)

These resources from Cook Communications Ministries are available through your local Christian bookstore.

Table of Contents

Acknowledgments

Words are a good vehicle to express feelings. Gail and I would like to express our feelings to a few beautiful people who have helped us on this journey.

First, to our friends and adopted family members Kurt and Olivia Bruner. You have been a real source of encouragement. You supply us with the impetus to work harder through sharing open doors. Thank you both.

To Jim Weidmann (a man's man), and to Janet Weidmann for your passion for family; we watch yours with intense intrest.

To Randy Scott who has a clear vision of what family life can and should be. Thank you for your inspirational spirit.

To Sherry Krigbaum, my secretary, for her awesome skills and untiring devotion to ministry.

To our friend Debbie Golden for an endless supply of resources and for reading the roughness out of the early manuscript.

To Lisa Rasmussen who encourages us to leave landmarks for others to follow.

To our editor, Marlee Alex, for her travail to fashion our thoughts into a purposeful manuscript.

To our lovely daughter-in-"love," Erika Joy, and our handsome son-in-"love," Justin Davis, for reminding us by their patience and presence how fortunate we really are.

Of course, we especially acknowledge our parents, Jack and Margaret Hover and Lloyd and Mimi Ledbetter, along with our grandparents, for giving us the legacy of freedom, a sweet and aromatic family fragrance!

Introduction

I was sitting in front of a microphone, my head down, absorbed in discussing the book, *Your Heritage,* that Kurt Bruner and I had recently completed. When I finished explaining how it is possible to break the cycle of pain that comes with a bad family legacy, I raised my eyes to meet the next question. To my shock the interviewer was wiping tears from her face. She then asked, "You mean I don't have to give my children what I was given? I was under the impression," she continued, "the pain that fell into my life would just tumble into my children's lives. I thought they, like me, merely have to make the best of it."

If you, too, are wondering, "How can I pass on what I didn't receive?", if you were handed a weak heritage, and you want to pass on a strong one, the answer is simple and straightforward: **you get by giving.** Concentrate on the giving, and in the process you will receive. An incredible principle? Yes, and a powerful one.

In *Your Heritage,* we write:

The Scriptures, at times, seem paradoxical. It goes against all rational reasoning to give something away so one might keep it. How is it if one will "let go" he can be kept from falling? Shouldn't it be "hold tight" and climb as high as you can? Everyone knows that in order to get to the top and be successful, one has to step on people's heads. What is this "consider others better than yourselves" (Phil. 2:3)? That is not sensible, yet when tried, it proves true.

Creating a heritage is much the same. The value of the heritage is not in the keeping but in the giving. It is not an entitlement, but an inheritance ready to be given away. When you are busy building, giving, and passing it on to the future generations, you may find that you yourself have received a heritage that you did not get from your parents. It is a heritage God has graced you with

because of your diligence to your children and obedience to Him.[1]
(See the Heritage Builders Concept on page 167.)

In the chapters of this book, we will identify one of the most effective and important ways that the heritage-passing process can take place: cultivating your family fragrance. You will learn not only what that means; you will also gain important insights on the "how to's" so that you may implement it in everyday life. We want to help you remember by using the acrostic AROMA. AROMA stands for:

A ffection
R espect
O rder
M erriment
A ffirmation.

In the following pages, we share stories with you that will bring you to an understanding of each characteristic. Then we discuss the principle behind the story and help you grip the intentional impact of each idea.

God bless you and give you joy as you read and use these thoughts to draw your family close.

※ Chapter 1 ※

The Essence of
Family Fragrance

I asked my secretary, Sherry, to stop by our house as she went home and drop off some things I had forgotten. She told me later what an impact that visit made on her.

Our house was filled with candlelight and warmth from the hearth-side fire. All our children were there—including married ones and their spouses—sitting on blankets on the floor or wrapped in afghans on the sofas. We were watching Monday Night Football. Everyone was holding a platter with a bowl of homemade soup, thick buttered bread, and slices of fruit. Conversation was flowing, and everyone was playful and boisterous, yet peaceful and relaxed. We invited Sherry to stay. She was tempted, but instead felt suddenly on a mission, as she told me later. She had a hard-working man and two little boys at home waiting for her. She quickly left us, and began to plan a different evening. She thought, Yes, I've got some canned soup, some French bread, and an apple or two. I'll get Brian to build a fire, and the boys can gather the blankets off their beds.

Sherry experienced our home the only way any of us experience home: through the five senses. The atmosphere—what Sherry heard and saw—all registered an image in her mind. She wanted to recreate it.

J. Otis

"[We are] fearfully and wonderfully made," wrote the psalmist (Psalm 139:14, KJV). Who, giving a little thought to the human body, would dare to disagree? Among other miraculous intricacies, God created an awesome way for us to communicate with each other—through the body's five senses: touch, taste, sight, smell, sound. Without these five senses, how could we experience the wonder of the created world or interact with one another? Experts say that under normal conditions you can:

* Feel the weight of a bee's wing falling on your cheek from less than half an inch away.
* See a small candle flame from thirty miles away on a clear, dark night.
* Smell one drop of perfume diffused through a three-room apartment.
* Taste .04 ounce of table salt dissolved in 530 quarts of water.
* Distinguish between 300,000 different color variations.[1]

The home, God's modeling studio

Family is also experienced through the five senses. Children sense the values of their home with incredible accuracy moment by moment. It is how they first pick up on and process the concept of family, and the place to which they belong. Humans, like every other species, learn by seeing life modeled before their eyes and sensing it through the four other windows of communication. The place God prepared for that kind of modeling to take place is not the church—as important as it is, nor the school, or children's clubs, or any government institution. God intended people to learn about life in their homes. A willful newborn eventually becomes a selfless parent by watching his own parents live in a loving manner.

Sometimes we travel to the coast—a three-hour drive—for a

family get-together. We usually go ahead of our grown children and call them when we arrive, letting them know where the road repairs, detours, and speed traps are so that they can avoid them if possible. We tell them where a new restaurant may have opened, and if it's worth a stop. It's not that we are more intelligent than they, just that we have been there first. We have experience on that road and want to smooth the rough spots for them—encouraging them on the journey. We want them to enjoy the good things!

In a similar way, parents care for their children by sharing where they have encountered life's detours and chuckholes. They encourage their children by creating a family fragrance that draws them in and makes home a safe place to encounter those obstacles. It is through the senses that an overpowering desire is created within the human soul to stay connected with home, or to separate and remove oneself.

It is through the senses that an overpowering desire is created within the human soul to stay connected with home.

Each child has a permanent memory bank. Even infants pick up on what is going on in the home, immediately tagging their impressions and registering them through their senses into their imaginations. That is why it is important to intentionally create an atmosphere to which children will respond positively, one they will want to pass on to the next generation. An atmosphere left to itself, one that just happens, may not be all you want it to be. It may leave a void in a child's emotional health.

Sylvester Stallone describes his early life in New York City, where from the time he was two years old he lived with a hired caregiver in a boardinghouse. He visited his parents on weekends.

My parents had their difficulties so there wasn't any time for me or my younger brother. It wasn't a tranquil household. There was great chaos. My father was an extraordinarily exacting man, and if what you did wasn't a photocopy of the way he did it, then you had no abilities and had to be chastised and corrected. And quite often the correction was, you know, shocking. He made me feel extraordinarily inept. "Why can't you be smarter?" "Why can't you be stronger?" I didn't have one virtue. He never said he was proud of me.[2]

What about time and tranquility? A sense of cooperation and pride? Is that what you would like for your family? A caring aroma that is inviting and inspiring can be created with a little time, effort, and creative thinking. How can you create an intoxicating family atmosphere in your home? How can you draw your children in?

As our children grew, we wanted to continue to set the stage of home as a place they enjoyed and wanted to come to often. The scene we shared with you at the beginning of this chapter isn't limited to two-parent families, or just to families with children. Donna is a single mom successfully raising a son and two daughters. Although the eight-hour weekday coupled with a forty-five-minute drive home in the Los Angeles traffic leaves her frequently exhausted, she still musters the energy to create an intoxicating atmosphere for the four of them. The kids don't see that she collapses into bed hours after they have been bedded for the night. But to Donna, nothing is more important than creating a warm family life. Their favorite evening is Thursday, her day off. The kids anticipate it even while they're at school. Each one takes a turn requesting a favorite meal. Donna says she has lots of help in the kitchen that evening also—they cook, talk, and sing. It gives Donna a chance to answer questions and listen to endless, excited chatter. Candles flicker. The smell of potpourri from the family room, mixed with the aromas of cooking, works its magic.

Even if there is just one parent or two adults and no children in your home, don't discount the importance of atmosphere. It can easily pick up spirits sagging from some loss, or encourage a spouse as you adjust to life together.

Smell, vanguard of the senses _____

The more prominent senses like sight and sound get greater press than the others. But it might surprise you to know that the sense of smell is the vanguard of the senses. Think of it!

Whatever we cannot see, taste, touch, or hear is recognized and interpreted through our nose. There are only three genes in each cell that control eyesight, but one thousand genes in each cell to control the sense of smell. Experts say that the nose can differentiate between ten thousand aromas. As the most direct sense, it can immediately enter the inner core of the brain which governs the emotions.[3]

In this book we identify and develop the heritage-building process in families using the idea of fragrance. You will gain insight into creating family atmosphere as we explore the acrostic *AROMA:* Affection, Respect, Order, Merriment, and Affirmation. Aroma has proven to soothe head and other body aches, insomnia, and high blood pressure. It relieves the mind of tension and depression, and even helps our moods. The incredible power of fragrance is the reason we chose the word *aroma* to describe the atmosphere that can be created in your family and home. But this recognition that aromas have a distinct affect on all the other senses is nothing new.

One has only to open the Scriptures to see how effectively the power of scent was used by the ancient Hebrews, or should we say, by Jehovah? Fragrance is first encountered in the Bible in the book of Genesis. God is considering the effect of the flood and is reacting to the burnt sacrifice that Noah and his family have offered. Listen to what the Holy Spirit moved Moses to write: "And the Lord smelled a soothing aroma. Then the Lord said in His heart, 'I will never again curse the ground for man's sake . . . nor will I again destroy every living thing as I have done'" (Genesis 8:21, NKJV).

Catch the power of that statement, then look again at what preceded the action: a soothing aroma. In our culture we would

Aroma has proven to soothe head and other body aches, insomnia, and high blood pressure. The incredible power of fragrance can be created in your family.

say, "When you said that, you made me *look* bad," or "*sound* bad." The image is most often perceived in the context of sight or hearing. Have you ever heard someone say, "What you said made me *smell* bad"? Probably not. But the Hebrews did. They used *aroma* to convey their emotions.

A conversation between Moses and the leaders of the children of Israel is recorded in Exodus. The men are miffed because Moses spoke harshly to Pharaoh and they feared that they may pay a price for that. "May the Lord look upon you and judge you," they say to Moses. "You have made us a *stench* to Pharaoh and his officials" (Ex. 5:21, NIV).

Solomon used a similiar analogy when he was warning against vulgar fun. Folly, he said, when it outweighs wisdom and honor, becomes a *smell* like bad perfume (Ecc. 10:1).

On several occasions in the New Testament, Christ's love for us and offering of Himself is likened to a "sweet smelling *aroma*" or "fragrant offering" to Jehovah (Eph. 5:2, NKJV). The Apostle Paul talks about the atmosphere we create when we live our lives before believers and unbelievers alike: "But thanks be to God, who always leads us in triumphal procession in Christ and through us spreads everywhere the *fragrance* of the knowledge of him. For we are to God the *aroma* of Christ among those who are being saved and those who are perishing" (2 Cor. 2:14-15, NIV).

What a beautiful statement! This is who we are and what we do! Read further in verse 16 as he describes the responses to this aromatic atmosphere: "To the one, we are the *smell* of death; to the other, the *fragrance* of life" (2 Cor. 2:16, NIV). Are there any doubts about the aroma we are empowered in Christ to create?

So remain intentional _____

In our homes, we receive a mixture of lovely and smelly family aroma. Nobody is perfect, and there are no perfect families. It is not *all* good or *all* bad. There will be times when disagreements will turn into squabbles, or when our ideal meal for the occasion isn't in the cupboards. We can almost guarantee that children will come close to sabotaging some of our best efforts at the worst possible times. But coming short of our goal for one day should not deter our efforts for the next day. If a sweet aroma is to be accomplished, it will take a determined focus on our part. It will require an intentional effort.

Although the following scenarios are black and white, we include them to give you a vivid picture of family fragrance. After reading each, think about how your senses are responding. How might you experience and describe these case studies by describing what you see, hear, feel, smell, taste?

It is loud. Noisy. There is yelling and arguing. The differing of opinions is obviously driving the chaos that is beginning to shape the parameters of "the game" that is going on in the room. The rules of "the game" are obvious. The one who can yell the loudest, the one who can block out all other opinions, the one who can ignore the feelings of all the others and can cut the deepest, will be the self-declared winner. But actually he will become an unwary loser. He will be a loser because this "game" isn't over. In fact, it has just begun. There will be payback time, and all involved know it and are waiting for it. The atmosphere is set for another confrontation. It may be tomorrow, or the next day, or even next week, but it will happen. The clouds created today are bulging with words yet to be said. They are dark and thick with hurt. The stage has been set. The characters are more than ready with their lines.

Were you to describe the responses of your senses, you might describe them like this:

Touch—sharp and cutting. Sound—dissonant and harsh. Taste—leaves a bitter residue. Sight—dark, off-center, twisted. Smell—pungent, nauseating.

Now try the same with this scene:

It is loud. Noisy. There is loud talking and laughter. The difference of opinion is coated with a healthy dose of respect and doesn't seem to matter much. Bright clouds are forming, bursting with affirming words to be said and stories to be told. There is anticipation that is infectious and merry. The game serves to strengthen the bond being built for future days. The clouds over this home are only there for shade. The stage is set. The characters can hardly wait for the next showing of this family gathering.

How did you sense it? You may be tempted to dismiss the contrast as "Pollyannaish." But confrontation and difference of opinions are not precluded in the latter example. The words are simply insulated by a healthy dose of affection. When affection permeates the atmosphere, most anyone can be confronted and anything discussed. Different opinions coated with affection somehow make them easier to swallow.

C.S. Lewis writes, "We can say anything to one another. The truth behind this is that Affection at its best wishes to say whatever Affection at its best wishes to say, regardless of the rules that govern public courtesy; for Affection at its best wishes neither to wound nor to humiliate nor to domineer."[4]

What is the difference between the two scenarios above? In the former, individuals seek to domineer and wound, while in the latter they seek to foster affection and affirmation "at its best." The importance of creating an atmosphere of affection and affirmation can't be overstated.

Mood replacement therapy _____

> **PRINCIPLE:** Family fragrance is not contingent on our family members' temporary moods or behavior.

> **INTENTIONAL IMPACT:** To kindle a permanent light of love that will burn consistently in our home.

Tom and Jennifer have worked out a way to help each family member become aware of negative mood swings. Since their children weren't immediately aware of when they were stuck in a bad mood, Jennifer devised a way of harmlessly bringing it to their attention. She made some "mood replacers" out of yarn. They looked like a bad model of the cookie monster. But when a negative mood was being sustained and nursed by a family member, someone would fetch a "mood replacer" and give it to the offender. It was a fun and harmless way to take the edge off and to come back to reality.

Family fragrance is not dreamy-eyed sentimentality. What we want our family members to feel when they pull into the driveway of our home is a reality so inviting, they can't wait to get inside

The teachers at the Christian high school where I (Gail) teach have a saying that works well at home, too. We should be "fair, consistent, and predictable." That does not leave out the qualities of mystique that add interest, but it does rule out mood swings that may make children wonder or worry if Dad or Mom is going to be in a bad mood from a tough day at work. Family members need to be able to rely on the fragrance in their home to be consistent and predictable. That doesn't mean parents have to pretend to always be *up* or put on a false happy face. Nor should we mask hurt and "stuff it." That later results in explosions of rage, or degenerates into depression.

Predictability does mean that we don't "take it out" on our children or spouse if someone else has gotten us riled up. There are issues at work in our home that are more important than "my feelings" or "my rights." Issues like love and duty, work and rest, peace and simplicity are based on God's love for us and we have an unwavering obligation to pass them on! Creating a soothing fragrance in our homes, we face a multitude of choices that require maturity. Family fragrance is not dreamy-eyed sentimentality. We can *choose* to forgive or hold a grudge. We can *choose* to overlook what we consider to be an injustice or make mountains out of molehills. We can *choose* to lovingly confront or plot to take revenge.

So what do we do with our moods? How do we handle a bad day when we feel like we have been beaten down unfairly? Where can we get help? The perfect model is Jesus. When He sensed the quick downswing of the moods of the disciples after He notified them that He was leaving, Jesus changed the atmosphere with some fragrant words: I want you peaceful, untroubled, and unafraid (John 14:27), he indicated. He gave them some "mood replacement therapy" by affirming what they already knew to be true: He would never leave them comfortless. Look again at His words:

✳ **Be Peaceful**—by believing He is in control. Jesus did not offer His disciples a worldly absence of conflict. He offered them HIS peace—a peace that has God at its center and His will in control. Jesus knew the problems His men were destined to face and He did not want them to view life's chaotic circumstances as master of their lives.

✳ **Be Untroubled**—by dwelling on His peace. We become troubled when we dwell on the unknowns and the "what ifs" of every circumstance. The underlying message from Jesus' statement is to dwell on "My peacefulness." A troubled spirit only serves to deepen trouble itself.

* **Be Unafraid**—by having a heart of faith. Dwelling on uncertainties and problems leads to eventual acquiescence to fear. Fear rushes to the chair where faith once sat. Fear blocks potential faith and steals our serenity.

So when you find yourself running on empty and sense a negative mood coming on, think on being peaceful, untroubled, and unafraid. Let these serve as your "mood replacers." Add them to your family fragrance by intentionally reminding yourself and your children of Jesus' words that circumstances should not dictate one's mood.

It isn't our intent to write a treatise on the discipline of behavioral patterns. While we understand that each family will encounter its own unique battles with strong-willed children or the erratic behavior of the early teen years, we believe that a sweet fragrance is still possible through it all. The process should not be given up because the child seems unresponsive to it. On the contrary, the process should be honed and intensified. The next five chapters are intended to help you in that process. We wish that you will create an atmosphere to which all will be drawn.

The glow from inside

Thomas Kinkade has become one of the most popular artists of our time, and it's no wonder. His pictures exude love and warmth, belonging and cheer, caring and detail. Like a large, jolly innkeeper of days gone by, they always greet us with a loud "Welcome!" We want to step inside one of his cottages or warm churches, and join in. Someone has always left the lights on for us. Even his evening pictures are aglow with gaslights. We always want to peek in the windows, know-ing we'd love to be a part of what's going on inside.

If we could use only one word to describe his paintings, some might choose beauty, warmth, loving, or belonging. But I would con-tribute the word hospitality, that invitation to join in simply because one has dropped by, urged to join in whether the home is ready for "company" or not. One will be accepted here. Those inside will always thin the soup, heat up more bread, cook another vegetable, and set another place. Kinkade's pictures don't make me sober, or reflective, teary-eyed, or sentimental. They make me want to find a time capsule and be "beamed up" into one of them.

Gail

Atmosphere is the light that glows from inside a home. What we want our family to feel when they pull into the drive-way of our home is the anticipation of love, warmth, beauty, and belonging that exudes from Kinkade's paintings. We want the feeling to be so inviting, the family can't wait to get inside. We hope that as you sit alongside us and our three children, you will get excited about the potential of your family's personal legacy. We hope you will get intentional about passing it on.

» Chapter 2 «

Affection
Is the Foundation
of Aroma

Affection

Respect

Order

Merriment

Affirmation

*T*he beloved disciple, John, wrote, "We love him, because he first loved us" (1 John 4:19, KJV). God's love for us was modeled by Jesus throughout the four Gospels. His love for children and His care for the physical welfare of those He healed, as well as His unqualified devotion for His disciples, speak volumes to those acquainted with His kingdom. Jesus asked His people to love one another. God's love culminated in His life offered on the Roman cross outside the walls of Jerusalem.

> *If love is the noun, affection is the verb*

I'm not sure we can ever in this life come close to identifying and describing the depth of Jesus' love for us. The joy and pleasure of existing with His Father in eternity was not more important than His deep need to redeem us by His love. We can plumb its depths, but we can never get to the bottom of it. Therefore, as He modeled such love for us, if we live close to Him, our homes should mirror the power of that love. When that love has taken root in the hearts of a family, it is consistently manifested in an outward show called affection. Perhaps within the family unit we might say *love* is the noun and *affection* is the verb.

Affection
is a consistent, loving act of the will, openly and sometimes spontaneously displayed toward its recipients.[1]

Affection is not manipulation for favors, nor is it a temporary display used for posturing in a relationship. It should not be used to get one's way. Affection is to be motivated by love and generated by an act of the will. Jesus said it best: "If ye love them which love you, what thanks have you? . . . I say, love your enemies" (Luke 6:32,35 KJV). The fragrance of our homes must be loving and affectionate simply because Jesus asked us to love one another.

Affection comes wrapped in skin _____

PRINCIPLE: Affection needs no reason, only someone to receive it.

INTENTIONAL IMPACT: To distribute affection equally, but not necessarily identically, to each member of our family.

In a Sunday School class we were helping to teach, our co-teacher, Gary, and his wife, Susie, were expecting a child. It would be their fifth. They were "jazzed" with the prospect, and their enthusiasm rubbed off on the staff as well as the sixty or so college students attending the class. As the due date drew nearer, the usual comments were heard: jokes about the delivery, the gender, the number of children already, the age appropriateness of the parents. And if you know college students, some of the comments were right on the edge.

The day arrived.

The unexpected happened.

The baby was born with severe deformities.

Gail and I were crushed. We cried at the news. We prayed for our friends. Sunday was approaching, and it would be Gary's time to teach. He asked me to take the class that morning, but wanted to say a few words first.

On Sunday, the class was somber. The usual bustle of energy was understandably gone. Gary got up to speak.

"I have felt your prayers this week," he started, "and they are always appreciated. Susie and the baby are fine. I feel so blessed."

"So blessed!" I thought. "He must be in denial!"

"Out of all the people in Southern California, God chose me to receive one of His special kids," Gary continued. "She can't respond to me; she doesn't know how. She may never know how. But I can love her. And I do love her . . . because she belongs to me. Nothing has taught me more about the love of God than she. And she has taught it in just a few days."

J. Otis

We can model the life of Christ in our affection to our children. Loving because someone deserves it doesn't work. Sooner or later that kind of love will shipwreck. Frequently, it leads to comparisons between siblings or outright favoritism on the part of one or both parents. Comparing beauty, athletic prowess, talent, intellect, or personality (such as a strong-willed vs. a compliant child) is destructive for the child who comes up short. The model God gave us is that affection does not need a reason, only an object. We needn't have His omniscience (all-knowing nature), but we do need a mature attitude and a will to show affection to our children for no other reason than that they belong to us.

> *"At home, I was the 'in-crowd,"* Becky says. *"The important people had saved me a seat. Their love for me made adolescent snubs unimportant."*

Gail once asked Becky, our second born, what she liked best about coming home—especially after being at school. Becky laughed at first because she disliked "tests" which required one right answer. But this question was easy once she realized she was being asked how she *felt* about coming home. "I couldn't wait!" she said. If anyone says the word "party," Becky immediately looks for the noisemakers and hats. But that often set her up for rejection by peers, if those she perceived as the "in-crowd" didn't save her a seat at the lunch table, on the bus, or in the stands. In reality, she was a typical teen who wanted acceptance.

"But going home, I belonged!" Becky says now. "I was the 'in-crowd.' The important people had saved me a seat, were ready to listen to my chatter, or tousle my hair. Their love for me made adolescent snubs unimportant. What is significant today as a young married woman is not that I was head cheerleader, homecoming princess, or an honor student in my graduating class, but the warm memories of my home with my siblings and parents. They gave me the ability to love others because they loved me."

Even when Rebecca's behavior stretched our disciplinary skills, it never altered or diminished our affection for her. Our intention was, and still is, to create a place where she, her siblings, and their friends could experience overwhelming affection.

Affection follows the will _____

> **PRINCIPLE:** When my relationship priorities are in order. my will acts accordingly.

> **INTENTIONAL IMPACT:** To express my affection in such a way that it will take root and influence the behavior of my children.

Stan had reached the age that is golden to every teen—the age of the driver's license. His father, Jack, took him aside to instruct him on reasons to be careful, and the consequences of not looking out for other drivers' intentions or lack of attention.

Having the lecture under his belt, Stan began to stretch his wings with his newfound source of freedom. He didn't do too badly. Jack reported on several occasions that his son seemed to be observing all the proper precautions of his recent "Mario Andretti" experiences.
Then it happened!

While in a corporate meeting, Jack was called from the room with the bad news that Stan had been in an accident. He was told the car was messed up pretty badly. Stan was fine, but shaken. Jack excused himself from the meeting and headed to the intersection where the accident happened.

A traffic accident has a way of consuming every emotion inside us. The trauma of it makes every nerve shake with the "what ifs" and the "if onlys." Running through Stan's mind were the many horror stories of how his friends' dads had reacted in the same situation. Based on those, he didn't want his dad to ever arrive. Stan wanted to curl up in a fetal position and make the world go away.

When Stan's dad pulled up to the wreck, he took not even a glance at the car sitting half on and half off the street. The crumpled metal didn't distract him. Jack didn't go over and bemoan the loss. From the moment he slid out of the driver's seat, Jack's eyes were fixed on his son. Jack walked straight to Stan and then embraced him until he stopped shaking. Jack took care of the paperwork and drove Stan home.

"As far as I know," related Stan, "Dad never once fretted over the vehicle. He only told me that a car is a tool. That I was important."
J. Otis

There was no doubt in Stan's mind where his dad's affections were—he was number one; his worth was never questioned by his father. From that moment, in that crisis, when most things might rush into a blur, Stan never questioned his dad's love for him. Jack had made order in his priorities years before, and under pressure, his will acted accordingly. The effects were permanently recorded in his son's memory bank. The residual affect of the scenario between Jack and his son will spill over into everyday life in their home.

Unconditional love evokes a response. As Stan trusts what his dad does and says, it translates into marked improvement in the atmosphere of the home. A tower of trust is built by Jack and his son. Because Jack's affection is outwardly visible to Stan, each occasion serves as another brick mortared into that tower of trust. Because of that trust, what Jack says and does is palpable. Stan finds himself responding in kind. Children respond to parents because with an act of our will, we first love them and show affection. Love and affection always alter behavior.

Theodore Roosevelt, our nation's twenty-sixth president, also grew up in an affectionate and close-knit family. His mother called their family's uninhibited embraces "melts," and TR called his father "the ideal man," and recalled childhood Christmas celebrations as being "literally delicious joy." Soon after he entered Harvard, TR wrote his father: "I do not think there is a fellow in college who has a family that loves him as much as you all do me, and I am sure that there is no one who has a father who is also his best and most intimate friend, as you are mine."[2] TR's whole-hearted devotion to his own family life had its roots in his upbringing. Years later he made this reflection:

There are many kinds of success in life worth having. It is exceedingly interesting and attractive to be a successful business man, or railroad man, or farmer, or a successful lawyer or doctor, or a writer, or a president, or a ranchman, or the colonel of a fighting regiment, or to kill grizzly bears and lions. But for unflagging interest and enjoyment, a household of children, if things go reasonably well, certainly makes all other forms of success and achievement lose their importance by comparison.[3]

Planning the experience of affection ————

"Experience engineering" is a new idea used in corporations to enhance business by helping clients tap into the sensory experience of it. Businesses, large and small alike, are encouraged to add a touch of God's greenery by placing topiaries by the entrance, or to catch the eye of a customer by having orderly, attractive thematic displays. And while eyes are occupied with color-coordinated visuals, the experts want noses to be just as busy. What customers smell or don't smell makes an indelible impression. Experts say use lamp rings and fragrant oils, fragrance in the restrooms, and light a pleasant-smelling candle in a safe place.

Next comes the sense of taste. Business owners are encouraged to tantalize tastebuds with simple treats. On special occasions, they offer a beverage or specialty coffee in small cups. Then fill senses with sound, experts suggest. Use a bell on the entry door. Answer the phone courteously. Refer to the customer's name often. It is simple to convey respect and value; these things make the buyer want to linger a while in the store. In this way, owners win customers' affections.[4]

Why not apply these principles in our homes to woo the affections of family members? If we fill our homes with the beautiful smells, sights, tastes, and sounds of happiness, and add the physical and non-physical elements of affection, then we are brewing up an intoxicating atmosphere. Children will desire to experience it over and over. Kids love to hear their name affectionately spoken from time to time, outside of being in trouble. Don't we all enjoy an encouraging wink from across the room, or an uplifting smile of approval when we enter?

Love pats and hugs for no particular reason, other than for just who we are, are always meaningful. As parents, we can create moods to make our children want to linger at home.

As parents, we can create moods to make our children want to linger at home.

Hugging is a learned behavior and a contagious act. When all around are receiving a hello or good-bye hug, no one wants to be left out, so most kids and adults will indulge. Some who have been raised without it may at first feel awkward, so get acquainted with it at your own pace and be patient with initiating others. Most signs of affection, like hugs, will cross gender lines, but of course, some do not. I doubt that our twenty-six-year-old son desires to sit on our laps anymore, but I hope my daughters will always want to sit close and snuggle.

If you grew up without these elements in your home, you may find yourself genuinely excited about starting, so let us urge you to begin. First, be honest with where you came from, where you want to go with your family fragrance, and what kinds of affection you want your family to experience. Next, be encouraged that you have within your power the ability to accomplish your vision. Then, be intentional. Create a plan of action and follow it to engineer that experience. You may be surprised at how creative you can become.

The Fragrance of Affection—Guidelines

To insure an affectionate atmosphere in the home, there are a few things to remember. Our fragrant guidelines are by no means exhaustive, but we think they will serve to point you in the direction you want to go.

1. Be sure that discipline of a child's bad behavior is not accompanied by withdrawal of your affection.

A distinction should be made because it is easy for a child, even a teenager, to become confused. Never allow your child to equate your rejection of his behavior as a sign that you don't love him. At the earliest stages of life, make statements like, "I love you with all my heart, but you will not be allowed to punch your little brother or scatter his toys." As he grows, you might put it this way, "Tom, I am upset you broke the window after we talked about not batting the ball toward the house. I will always love you, but your behavior is not acceptable and you'll have to be disciplined."

A child needs love the most when he is the most unlovable.

2. Model intentional affectionate acts in your home on a consistent basis.

It is amazing how a few planned, yet simply executed, acts can create a sweet aroma in your home. If your child has a bad day at school or on the playground, he may bring home a rotten attitude. You don't have to demand through clenched teeth, "You had better change your attitude around here, Bud!" You don't have to try and fix it by giving advice. A child needs love the most when he is the most unlovable. Why not try a glass of cold milk, a cookie, and a soft back rub? An arm around the shoulders? A vote of confidence in his abilities? Things like this will open the door for a little dialogue later. Our friend Debbie Golden has a wonderful way of celebrating the affection of her husband, two sons, and young daughter. After receiving fresh flowers and enjoying them, she hangs the flowers upside down in a dry place—usually in the kitchen. When dry, she makes them into potpourri. She may add perfumed oils to the petals, or mix them with other dried flowers. Small bowls of potpourri are placed throughout her home, and she has one huge glass urn that contains only rose petals. Sometimes she dries the long-stemmed roses from a special occasion as is, wraps them in patterned tissue, and ties the bouquet with beautiful ribbon. She places the entire cluster in a prominent spot.

3. Model and teach an affectionate servant's heart consistently in your home.

Someone said, "I'll know I have a servant's heart when I find others treating me like one!" This may be your biggest challenge in creating a fragrance of affection. Dad can model by helping in the kitchen after dinner, so Mom can join the family sooner. Mom might pitch in with yard work so Dad can have more time for the kids. Or perhaps the chores are reversed in your home. When children see their parents helping each other, they "get it." Modeled day in and day out, children pick up on unselfish attitudes. They begin to live them as well when serving is done in a spirit of affection and positive feelings. Having a servant's heart can be shown simply by one child helping another pick up his room so playtime comes sooner for both. We were pleased when our children began to help each other in this way, and blown away when Matthew cleaned and straightened Rebecca's entire closet one day.

Of course, there is a difference between a willing servant and an unwilling slave. We should not let our desire to be self-less and to willingly serve others be taken advantage of. Mom—or even Dad—and the oldest sibling aren't the only ones who are required to have a servant's heart. Yes, Jesus humbly washed the disciples' feet to teach them the lesson of serving others, but He also confronted the disciples many times during His earthly ministry. He was no doormat. If you want a house full of harmony, it is everyone's responsibility to learn to serve the others.

4. At every opportunity, say freely, "I'm sorry," and "Please forgive me."

After a misunderstanding between you and your children, "Please forgive me," seems to strike the heartstring of the offended. Use this when you've judged a child incorrectly, whether accidentally or after making a decision based on faulty information. Children need to see Mom and Dad quickly respond to each other with "I'm sorry," and "I was wrong," too.

And when your children model a servant's heart and repentance, even on a smaller scale than the prodigal in Jesus' parable, it's time to openly rejoice. In Tim and Diane's family, when the children were caught fighting, they were sent to the "Apology Stools." All sides of the story were listened to by a neutral authority. Each viewpoint was discussed. Then the children were expected to talk it out and apologize to each other. The discussion ended with an "I'm sorry," a hug, and (hopefully) a desire not to do it again.

Milder skirmishes can be interdicted with an "Okay, you're about to have to hug and kiss!" That gentle reminder usually gets the response, "Oh, yuck!" Laughter accompanies the end of fussing. Good feelings result when you let your child know she is loved and that she still belongs.

5. Model and teach an attitude of affectionate communication in your home.

They say, "A picture is worth a thousand words." When you model attitudes, you are becoming a picture for your children. You'll communicate to them what you may never be able to explain in words. What pictures come to your mind that you may live in front of your children when you hear the following words? Talk. Coo. Listen. Observe. Touch. Hug. Cry. Respond. Laugh. Agree. Challenge. Question. Answer. Cheer. Congratulate. Caress. Motivate. Play. Goof-off. Pray. Sing. Tickle. Rough-house. Joke. Share. Reminisce. Help. Respect. Give. Encourage. Love. How do these ideas stir images of affectionate behavior for you?

Do you want to open some important conversation? Do like the Randall family and mention a few of those words at the dining table throughout the week. Take one at a time. Ask the children to say what pictures it brings to mind. Ask if they think there is enough of that kind of affection in your home. Who would they like to get more from? The Randalls say this dialogue opened unusual communication by allowing the family to reveal hidden hurts and needs for affection.

6. Show your children how to keep personal priorities in order.

A great way to show you love your children is to sit down with them at appropriate milestones in their lives and discuss what's coming. Some milestones will be: the beginning of school, overnighters with people other than family, puberty, moving on to junior high and high school, the beginning of team sports, music or art lessons, youth activities, driving, or things like salvation, baptism, or the first time children partake in the Lord's Supper. Talk through what each milestone means, and how the children's lives will keep changing in the years ahead. Help them begin a list of possible priorities for the following twelve months. Find a way to show them that it is always easier to make quick decisions when a person's priorities have been contemplated. For instance, if studying a particular subject at school or learning to play a new instrument is high on a child's priority list, he will have a choice to make when something else tempting comes along. The ability to make the proper decision will be more clear-cut if he has rehearsed priorities in his own mind.

Doing this requires quality time with your child. The phrase "quality time" is confusing and overused. A friend of ours who audits films for television documentaries once told me that it takes two hours of film to get two minutes of quality shots. Quality only comes with quantity. Quality time with your child only comes out of quantity time.

It takes two hours of documentary film to get two minutes of quality shots; quality time comes only with quantity time.

7. Always remember, each child does not have to be treated with the same kind of affection.

Don't get blind-sided when your child yells, "It's not fair!" This phrase is a parenting trap, a catch-all statement kids use when they think they are getting left out or have somehow been short-changed. Affection in the home, a loving, consistent act of the will, does not mean treating everyone the same, but treating everyone according to his need. Not every child will be an "A" student, for example. Not all will be athletic or competitive. Not all will be neat dressers or musical or articulate. You're getting the idea. Since our children are not the same, our expectations of each one will be different. It is important to affectionately encourage each child toward his particular bent. We are not saying to love one child above another. We are saying, dwell with each child according to knowledge. One may not respond to kisses and hugs. Another may need lots of them. One may need high fives and slaps on the back. Learn how to show affection in the way a child understands and accepts it best.

⌽ Fragrant Tips from Gail ⌽

Affectionate interaction with children, toddlers to adolescents, is important throughout each day. But the most important moments, I believe, are the way you wake up children in the morning, and how you put them to bed at night. J. Otis touched on this in *Your Heritage* when he humorously contrasted how he handled the children's bedtime with the way I did:

My style was to holler to the kids, "You kids better get in that bed—or I'm going to jail for homicide!" In the Ledbetter home, I tried to get them up in the morning with sensory overload: flash the overhead light on and off, sing loudly and off-key, and irritate them out of bed and into a lousy mood. Gail decided maybe it would be better if she came up with a more composed way.[5]

Starting the day—awakening

Waking my children was one of my favorite times of day. When our two oldest were small, they shared a room. About ten minutes or so before I wanted them to get up, I would turn over the Ethel Barrett LP to which they fell asleep listening the night before. It was usually a story with some good music or a cassette: "Down By the Creek Bank" or "The Music Machine" that taught the fruits of the Spirit. (Does that bring back memories, or what?) Once they had come out of a deep sleep and were dozing with eyes closed, I would sit on their beds, rub their backs, and slide my hand down the side of their faces. I'd softly say, "It's time to get up. Today your class is going to the science fair." They were soon ready to get out of bed. I heard them say many times how it made an impression on them to wake up feeling loved, secure, and looking forward to the day.

With Matt and Becky, I was more or less just feeling my way. I got intentional with our youngest, who came along nine years after Becky. In the winter months, I still go into fifteen-year-old Leah's room early and turn over her music cassette. I may light her fragrance candle, raise her window shade a few inches, or turn on a low-watt bulb. She enjoys waking up slowly, and knows that she doesn't have to get up until I come in again. About ten minutes later, I return with hot chocolate or another beverage. I rub her face, and she always smiles before she opens her eyes (like her older sister). She usually hugs my hand by scrunching up her shoulder. She has even kissed my hand. All of this may take only five minutes, but I can't think of anything more valuable. Because each child knows he or she is loved, this short ritual has rid our home of countless arguments, retorts, moodiness, and ungrateful attitudes. It starts the day off on an affectionate note.

Ending the day —bedtime

Reading together is the last thing I did with the children after brushing teeth and other hygiene rituals. We always read from beautifully illustrated books when the children were young. (We have every book that artist Tasha Tudor has ever done.) As they grew older, lights could stay on and they read on their own if they chose to. Our routine wasn't a compulsion; we never read on Sunday or when they had a long or difficult day. Bedtime was not allowed to be a battle-ground or an exercise of wills. Instead, the day ended peace-fully and contentedly—and intentionally. The children looked forward to bedtime, were not plagued with fears, and I'm sure were able to rest better than if bedtime had been difficult.

Once the children were happily in bed, I could get some work done! My energy level was not sapped by emotional wrangling. I could focus on creative things, not rehearse angry feelings. My kids were not perfect, and neither was I. We had some difficult nights at times, but arguing about waking up and bedtimes was not a way of life. Parents can choose to live in chaos and frustration, and can choose to act as though they can't do anything about it. Doesn't family strife just seem like such a waste of time? Instead of the con-temporary saying, "The Force is strong in my family," let the children be able to say to their friends, "The force of Love is strong in my family."

. . . . .

Recommended Books:

Bedtime for Frances, Russell Hoban
Amelia Bedelia, the series, Peggy Parish
The Forgetful Bears, Lawrence Weinberg
Mother, Mother, I Want Another, Maria Polushkin
Love You Forever, Robert Munsch
Through Grandpa's Eyes, Patricia MacLachlan
Little Visits With God, Allan Jahsmann &
    Martin Simon

Miss Nelson is Missing, James Marshall
Blueberries for Sal, Robert McCloskey
I'm Terrific, Marjorie Weinman Sharmat
Alexander and the Terrible, Horrible, No Good,
        Very Bad Day, Judith Viorst
When I Was Young in the Mountains,
        Cynthia Rylant
Winnie the Pooh, A. A. Milne
The Book of Virtues, William J. Bennett
The American Girls Collection, the series,
        Pleasant Company
Night Light Tales, Andy Holmes
Devotions for the Sandbox Set, Jane Morton
Kingdom Parables, Christopher Lane

. . . . .

Remember, as often as possible, affect all five senses:

Waking Up Your Children

Taste: Hot chocolate, orange juice
Smell: Scented candles, cinnamon tea, cocoa
Touch: Back, brow, and face rubs
Sight: Someone who treasures them as soon as they
        open their eyes
Sound: Your voice, talking with love

Going to Sleep

Taste: Ice-cold water (or a snack and then teeth brushed)
Smell: Soap from clean bodies, body lotions, scented
        candles
Touch: Caresses and kisses
Sight: A family who loves them
Sound: Your voice, soft music, *Odyssey* tapes, etc.

Family nights

At the beginning of chapter one, we related a story about my husband's secretary stopping by, and what she felt when she entered our home. I've been asked on several occasions to share tidbits on how to create an inviting home. Let me share how I intentionally created the atmosphere that night.

I laid the big cotton quilt on the floor and draped afghans over the sofa and chairs for nestling. Leah brought in extra pillows. J. Otis started the fire. I lit the candles. During the football season, and especially after the nation goes back to standard time, darkness falls early. I use lots of candles, especially scented ones, generously placing tapers and stubby ones of all sizes in our public rooms, even bathrooms. (Watch for sales; candles are one of your cheapest mood setters.) Sometimes, just for my own enjoyment, I turn the kitchen lights off and cook an entire meal by candlelight.

. . . . .

Candles are one of your cheapest mood setters

. . . . .

Sun tea was steeping all day, and I started the soup early so that simmering would blend the flavors. Arriving home from work, I started the breadmaker. The smell of just-baked bread was at its peak when everyone arrived, and fresh oranges were sliced and ready at the same time. That way everyone was sure to get the full impact of the luscious scent. Quickly, I added slices of green and red apples dipped in lemon juice (to prevent discoloring) to the fruit platter.

When everything was ready, I stood back to see if all I had intentionally created said, "I love you."

Now some of you are saying, "No way, I hate football!"

But reconsider a moment. If you take something away from your menfolk that is important to them, the vacancy may be too big for you to fill with something else. I say, "If you can't beat 'em, join 'em." If you don't have family, invite friends over. Maybe the ladies can go to the kitchen for something they enjoy, but if you do stay together, ask questions about the game. The men will find them hilarious and entertaining. The point is to take any occasion to make a memory—even if it is not your favorite thing.

. . . . .
I stood back to see if all I had intentionally created said, "I love you."
. . . . .

Menu for Fun

Taste: Potato cheese soup, buttered bread, sliced fruit
Smell: Yeast bread, oranges, simmering soup, scented candles
Touch: Cotton, wool, over-stuffed pillows
Sight: Flickering flames, starlight through windows
Sound: Crackling fire, engaging conversation

A Tussie Mussie

Would you like to carry on a Victorian tradition of communicating your affection? A tussie mussie (tuh-see muh-see) is a holder for cut flowers, about the size of a pointed sugar cone. Used before paper was plentiful or telephones were commonplace, they signified, according to the flower sent, romantic interest or friendship. Simple ones might be made from paper or heavy cardboard; others were made from tin, brass, or sterling silver. Today they can be found in antique stores or specialty gift shops.

In Victorian days, flowers were declarations of affection: the flowering almond signaled hope, the calla lily declared magnificent beauty, and the cedar leaf meant "I live for thee." A lady may have returned the tussie mussie with a daffodil, expressing regard or a garden daisy meaning "I share your sentiment." A wild daisy would have meant "I will think on it." The purple lilac expressed first emotions in love. Perhaps her suitor then may have sent lemon blossoms conveying fidelity. Friends or servants would carry the exchange of affection back and forth in the tussie mussie. They were not only used for romantic purposes. Friendship greetings were exchanged in the same way. Zinnias meant "thoughts of absent friends," and sweet basil "good wishes." Rhubarb would say "I need your advice."

You can buy, or make and decorate, your own tussie mussies. Books are available explaining the meanings of flowers, or you can come up with your own from the foliage you have available. Upper elementary and junior high school girls will enjoy the secrecy and exclusivity involved.

Table Talk or Car Chat

Try asking questions like these at the dinner table or in the car while you are on a trip or on the way to school. Remember to be open, and don't ask a question if you really don't want to know the answer.

Describe affection using only the sense of smell and taste.

How can affection be shown without words?

Reach over and touch your brother's/sister's or Mom's/Dad's face in a way that will demonstrate affection.

How can we demonstrate affection through giving?

What does Mom/Dad say or do for you that makes you feel loved?

Since God is not physically present, how does He show His affection toward us?

Share a Journal

Start a journal to be shared exclusively with one or each of your children. Make an entry, telling your child a story, something about your past, what happened that day, or about a current subject. Place the book under her pillow. Now it is her turn to write something. When she is finished, she can place it under your pillow. Each entry should be dated. There is no rush; it may be exchanged every two or three days, once a week, or sporadically. It can be a wonderful way to express feelings, and will greatly improve everyone's writing skills!

Chapter 3

The Pleasures
of Respect

A*ffection*
R*espect*
O*rder*
M*erriment*
A*ffirmation*

*In first grade, Mr. Lohr said my purple teepee wasn't realistic
enough, that purple was no color for a tent, that purple was a
color for people who died, that my drawing wasn't good enough to
hang with the others. I walked back to my seat counting the swish-
swish-swishes of my baggy corduroy trousers. With a black crayon,
nightfall came to my purple tent in the middle of the afternoon.*

*In second grade, Mr. Bara said, "Draw anything." He didn't care
what. I left my paper blank, and when he came around to my desk, my
heart beat like a tom-tom while he touched my head with his big hand
and in a soft voice said, "The snowfall. How clean and white and
beautiful."*

*Every child is an artist. The problem is how to remain an artist
once he grows up.*[1]

Pablo Picasso

Respect entails many pleasures that arise from regard for life
and property, the world that God created, and the opinions and
rights of other people. But the family fragrance is never more
pleasant than when each family member understands each

other's true worth. Each child contributes a personal ingredient that makes up the atmosphere of the home. If that unique value is doubted, or worse, stripped away, the entire family suffers. Without respect, a home can produce people with sassy mouths, self-righteous spirits, hurtful independent wills, and attitudes of "I don't need anybody," and "I can do it without you."

Family fragrance is never more pleasant than when each family member understands each other's true worth.

Showing respect for children not only helps them develop manners and a habit of courtesy, it inhibits destructive self-criticism, and will result in respect given back to peers, parents, or other adults. The biblical principle is: We get by giving (Luke 6:38). Any farmer understands the law of sowing and reaping (Galatians 6:7-9). Harvesting never comes before planting. A farmer doesn't expect to harvest anything but exactly what he plants. In between comes much watering, weeding, and controlling pests. It is the same with respect. A parent can't expect to harvest respect until respect is first planted, practiced, and nurtured in the home. When you make the effort to respect your children, your children will make the effort to respect others. Respect travels a two-way street; a youngster can't give it away if he has never received it. Children don't care how much you know until they know how much you care.

Respect
is holding other people in honor
so they may recognize their own true worth.[2]

Respecting life's ebb and flow

PRINCIPLE: A child's self-worth and attitude is built, brick by brick, on loving acts of respect in all circumstances.

INTENTIONAL IMPACT: To produce in our children respect for the balance of life's ups and downs.

Sherry came home from school dejected. She had failed a test and was "bummed" about her less than normal accomplishments. Her dad sat down beside her.

"Did you do your best?" he asked.

"Yeah."

"Did you prepare yourself?"

"Yeah."

"Well, what's the big deal?"

"What do you mean, Dad?" Sherry asked. "I failed the test. You and Mom are going to be disappointed."

"I'm proud of you because you are my daughter," her father told her. "I'm proud that you prepared and did your best. You won't ace every test in life; even big league ballplayers fail three out of four times they step to the plate. It's those three failures that make them want to get

back to the plate. Move on the next challenge."

Sherry went away with her shoulders back and a smile on her face.
J. Otis

A lecture with a scowl from Dad would have produced the opposite emotion and body language from Sherry. Had Dad taken the opportunity to point out what a jerk that teacher was for giving his daughter a bad grade, he would have undermined respect for the teacher's authority and for his own modeling at home. When things are going well, it is easier for children to show respect. But life ebbs and flows like the tide. Sometimes it's up, sometimes it's down. The reality is, not everything is going to go right all the time. That's why teaching a habitual practice of respect for yourself, along with courtesy and manners, is so important. Respect shown by attitudes toward the ebb and flow of life could well determine its quality. In daily situations where things are not going *our* way as parents, we have a practice field upon which to model a proper choice of attitude. With that foundation, our children can make attitude choices that will help them become better. Without it, they may become bitter.

Each child contributes a personal ingredient that makes up the atmosphere of the home.

When an attitude slippage is eminent because of a sour circumstance or a disappointing incident that may have occurred, stop and check your conversation and manners, Mom and Dad. See to it that due respect is upheld. Solomon said it best: "He who is slow to anger is better than the mighty, And he who rules his spirit than he who takes a city" (Prov.16:32 NKJV). Some families use buzz words to alert each other that a certain attitude isn't wholesome. For example, the Jostens use the word "battleship." If Bill is allowing a bad attitude to seep into conversation with his children, his wife Jill will say something like, "Battleship gray wouldn't look good on our car would it?" Bill hears the buzz word and without open rebuke realizes an adjustment is needed.

If you came from a home where respect and honor was not modeled, then a habit of courtesy and manners must be developed. How can this be accomplished? Have attitude checks with the family when the atmosphere gets thick with upsetting circumstances. One family teaches respectful attitudes by cassette tape. At the dinner table everyone is notified that the conversation is being taped for "quality control." Parents tell jokes and engage the children in fun conversation. Then for the novelty of listening to their voices later on the tape, their table-talk is captured. It is sometimes entertaining, and other times enlightening to the children when they hear how corrections are needed in their attitudes. "It is amazing," said Mrs. Linder, "how the children didn't realize and didn't like the way they whined or spoke disrespectfully." The tape became a non-judgmental teacher.

If either Gail or I detected a sassy or disrespectful attitude when our children were learning the aroma of respect, we would simply stop the conversation. One of us would say, "Let's start that sentence again." Then we would guide the sentence into the appropriate direction and proper wording. If we heard, "Pass the bread," we would say, "Could you try that again, please?" Then we would hear, "Oops! Would you pass the bread, please," and then a "Thank you."

Being generous with honor and respect goes deeper than

doing so only when a child is well-behaved. It reaches farther than accomplishments and performance. One girl shared that when she played on the softball team, she got a snow cone after the game when she got a hit, or when she hit a home run. But if she struck out, or flied out, all she got was the silent treatment or a "Why couldn't you do better?" lecture. This continued into her teen years in her relationship with boyfriends. Respect or honor was promised only after performance; if she did what they wanted, they would do what she wanted. Later, this young woman had difficulty believing that Jesus didn't require performance for His acceptance.

Honor and respect should come generously in spite of childish or adolescent behavior. We aren't saying that an honorable act should not receive a greater reward. We are saying that generous honor in any circumstance will give children a model to follow. Also, children will equate honor under any circumstance more with who they are, and not just with what they do or fail to do.

The two kinds of respect

PRINCIPLE: There is a difference between entitled respect and earned respect., usually appropriate at different, times, and occasionally appropriate at the same time.

INTENTIONAL IMPACT: To produce in our children respect for other people and property by showing respect for them and their property.

There was a time in our country when American military forces suffered a lack of respect. The nation's response to the Vietnam War stripped men and women of honor deserved as they served their country. My cousin Jerry had encountered the enemy in some of the worst fighting in Vietnam. Letters to his fiancée, Sheila, and his family expressed sadness and sorrow. At times, he implied he felt he might not make it home. Shortly before he was to return, his platoon had a fierce encounter with the enemy. The Viet Cong attacked and his company dropped to the ground. When the horror was over and Jerry made it back to base, his worst fears were realized—all of his buddies had been killed in the skirmish.

Sometimes it's up, sometimes it's down. That's why teaching a habitual practice of respect for yourself, along with courtesy and manners, is so important.

From that day, Jerry talked about coming home, but he knew he would be returning to a cynical country.

Abruptly, before he was able to wire information to his family, Jerry was shipped out and flying over the Pacific. He intended to call once on American soil, but had to run through the airport to make his connection. Jerry realized that after terrifying months of artillery, the sight of endless rice paddies, and the smell of death, no one would be at the airport in his hometown to greet him. When he arrived there Sunday morning, he grabbed his duffle bag, hailed a taxi, and headed for church where 6,000 people were about to begin the worship service.

Voices from the 400-seat choir loft began to sing. Jerry, still in uniform, made his way through the lobby. Like a man on a mission, he headed for the aisle at the right center where he and Sheila always sat *in the days he had courted her. He was soon spotted and his presence made quite a stir, catching the pastor's attention. The pastor interrupted the singing and announced, "Folks, Jerry is coming home from Vietnam, and I mean right now!"*

People turned and began to clap louder and louder. Sheila stood in shock and burst into convulsive sobs. The clapping, amens, and tears had become a roar. Finding his bashful sweetheart, he gathered Sheila in his arms and kissed her full on the lips in front of the cheering congregation. Some days later, they became man and wife.

Gail

Jerry's church poured out love and honor as this decorated soldier began a new phase of his life. Today Jerry speaks little of his time in Vietnam, but his place in the hearts of extended family and friends has never been questioned. Collectively and spontaneously they showed him the respect he had earned and to which he was entitled as a serviceman.

Distinguish between the two types of respect and teach both in your home. *Entitled* respect is when a person is due respect by virtue of position: a parent, employer, teacher, pastor, or peace officer. It has more to do with who you are than what you have done. Scripture gives honor to these positions and parents can model respect for them. Hold those in positions of authority in high regard, although they are not perfect. They may make misjudgments from time to time. By reacting to their misjudgment we can further break down communication and respect toward them—even giving children the idea that all authority is bad or stupid. It is easier to later explain a mistake made by an adult, than to rebuild respect that has been torn down by overreacting in anger or gossip.

Earned respect is when we give respect because of what someone has done or how someone has lived. We gain it through our labor, our service to others, and our performance within the family unit. Earning respect as I wrote in my book *Your Heritage* is drawn from the concept of two other words, *earnest* and *yearn*. The primary purpose of earned respect then is to strive with earnest effort and yearning to advance or stretch forward as a person.[3]

Gail and I wanted to inculcate in our children entitled respect for others' personhood and property and give the kids opportunities to earn respect for themselves. Sometimes when they did things for which we could have come down on them, we instead tried to make it a teachable moment. One day, for example, Gail noticed a twenty-dollar bill missing from her jewelry box. The only people who knew it was there were our children. I went outside where they were riding their bikes. I called Matt over. "Some money is missing from your mom's jewelry box," I said. "Do you know anything about it?"

I searched Matt's face for clues when he answered, "No."

Becky kept riding her bike back and forth, listening. I called her and asked the same thing. Before I finished, she blurted out, "What twenty dollars?"

"Becky, how did you know how much money was taken?" (I had never said how much.) Her dark eyes were flashing and darting back and forth. Although we still laugh about her guilt-ridden response, Gail and I took the time to explain how serious the offense was. We also allowed Becky to prove herself. She worked hard to *earn* the respect back that had been damaged.

The Fragrance of Respect–Guidelines

1. Be generous with family honor in life's ups and downs.

When a child is entitled to honor or has earned it, that fact should not be overlooked. Don't pass up opportunities to respond. Placing pictures on the refrigerator or hanging certificates of accomplishments in a prominent place says a great deal to a child. One family began a House of Honor made of Legos and placed it on top of the piano in their family room. Everytime anyone in the family demonstrated an act of kindness, it was honored by placing one Lego block in place to build the walls of a house. When the house is complete, the family is planning a trip to the coast to celebrate.

When their third daughter was diagnosed with scoliosis and placed in a full body cast, the Hovers moved Debby into the central-most area of their two-story home. They wanted to make sure she didn't miss any family time or spontaneous fun. Her siblings wanted Debby to feel she was important to their family by helping her be in the middle of things with life happening all around her.

2. Build up people around you, even those you disagree with.

If we ruin the influence of another adult with our children, we may negate any influence for good that person may have on our children in the future.

The major part of a pastor's time is, of course, taken up working with people. Usually the congregation and I share a mutual desire to move ministry forward in unity. But there are times when a person is in strong disagreement with my manner of administration. Disagreement in itself isn't a disqualifier for a relationship, but if I verbally disrespected another adult in front of my children or other adults, the children may personally disqualify anything that individual can potentially teach them. After all, a broken clock is even correct twice a day. Instead of running the risk of creating an environment for bitterness to seep into a life, if I can't say something positive, I say nothing.

3. Confront your child's self-criticism with positive input.

Self-criticism is different than self-evaluation. The first tears down, the second looks to build up. The former is negative, the latter is positive. When a child gets down on himself, it is often over some insignificant issue. When my son played on his high school basketball team, we faced this dilemma early. If he had a bad night on the court he would really get down on himself. Statements like "I'm no good," or "I think I'll quit" revealed his strong self-criticism. We tried to turn it into evaluation with suggested questions like, "Where were my mistakes?" and "How can I overcome them?" In the context of his entire life, simply pointing out a small failure early on can frequently end doubting.

4. Respect your children's privacy. Give them a place in your home that is solely theirs. Don't invade it without their permission.

Gail and I wanted our children to respect our privacy, so we respected theirs. We always knocked before entering the children's rooms. We never rifled through their chest of drawers to read notes and letters. Lack of respect of property is a form of thievery just like picking flowers from a neighbor's flower bed or "sharing" answers over a test in school. This can lead to cheating elsewhere.

Ali regrets the day she picked up her daughter's personal journal from her drawer and opened it. When Nichole found out, she quit writing her deepest thoughts for fear of it happening again. Ali realizes she stole her daughter's desire to express herself. It is regrettable, and Ali is working hard to assure her daughter that she will respect her privacy.

5. Avoid profanity in all conversations.

Profanity degrades people. Even when not aimed at anyone, it degrades the one who uses it. Scripture teaches that words should be used to uplift others. Profanity is a downward spiral that leads to baser things. A seven-word sentence Rhett Butler declared at the end of *Gone with the Wind* took weeks to get through censors in 1939. Today, the same word spoken by a preschooler frequently doesn't even warrant a frown. Don't allow the fragrance of your home to be polluted by profanity.

Children will bring words home they learn on the playground. There is always that child at school who feels it is his duty to inform the other children about crass words or phrases. It happened to our children. Several times! It is shocking to say the least. I practically fell out of my chair in hysterics. But Gail approached it with calm and a matter-of-fact demeanor. (I usually left the room.) Gail first wanted to know the who, where, and why of such a word. Then if an explanation was warranted, the child received it and the word was explained (unless vulgar or explicit) to the children. Proper instruction about language was then given, along with an admonition as to its non-use in our family.

Second chances show that a parent has enough confidence in a child's character to trust he will see a task or situation through a resolution.

> *"Where did you hear that word, Becky?"*
> *"At school, Mommy!"*
> *"Who told it to you?"*
> *"Bobby."*
> *"Why do you think he said it?"*
> *"I don't know."*
> *"What do you think it means?"*
> *"I don't know."*
> *"Well, it's not a word we use in our family so it's probably best that you not say it again."*
> *"Okay!"*

6. Be a parent of second chances.

God shows respect to His children through His mercy. We all learn by mistakes. Second chances show that a parent has enough confidence in a child's character to trust he will see a task or situation through to a resolution. An unforgiving parent will impede the child's learning processes.

One only has to be vaguely familiar with Israel's history to see this characteristic fleshed out. God consistently forgave and corrected Israel's course to match His plans. He told them through the prophet Jeremiah, "For I know the plans I have for you . . . plans to prosper you and not to harm you, plans to give you hope and a future" (Jer. 29:11, NIV). The Lord accomplished His perfect plan with imperfect people by being a God of second chances.

In the New Testament, Jesus illustrates this with Peter. Peter's impulsive temperament was consistently in need of second chances. He denied his Lord, sagged in his belief, and influenced others to give up. After the resurrection, when he encountered Jesus on the seashore, Peter sat silently, wondering about his status with the Lord, but afraid to ask. He was afraid that his unbelief would bring displeasure to God. The atmosphere must have been thick with emotion.

Jesus broke the ice by turning to Peter and asking, "Do you love Me . . . ?" (John 21:12-19 NKJV). Not an "I told you so." It was a beautiful question to affirm second chances. Then Jesus said, "Feed My lambs." Jesus left Peter's responsibility intact. Because Peter was prone to mistakes does not mean he was not a man after God's own heart. Second chances paid off. Peter became an enormous influence in the early church.

⪻ Fragrant Tips from Gail ⪼

When showing respect for your family, it takes little effort to be above average! Think about the business world and the service mentality that permeates the best restaurants in town. What about your favorite place to eat? Is it clean? Attractively decorated? What does it smell like? Does music add or detract from the atmosphere? Does the food look as inviting to the eye as to the palette? Is the waiter polite? Friendly? Is the service prompt and accommodating without being pushy? Is the general appeal gracious?

Restaurants strive for excellence because their bottom line is money. A successful business is one which rises above the pack in the effort to please. How much more important to strive for excellence for the sake of legacy. As a young home-maker, I learned it takes little effort to rise above the average, and rarely more money. The major requirement and invest-ment is creative thought and love, alongside an eagerness to serve. How will our children understand and appreciate their worth if we don't show them by making an effort to honor them? I'd love to hear some of your creative ideas to honor family. Here are some of mine:

Mealtimes

Determine to sit at a table during mealtimes, and be sure
everyone joins. Turn off the television. The greatest gift you
can give your family is you. Talk. Converse. Share. Laugh.
Don't make it a time for correcting a child's bad behavior or
discussing problems. Children should look forward to mealtimes.

Set the Table Beautifully

Prepare to dine, not just eat. Use your best for everyday.
People treat nice things with respect and that often translates
into more respectful behavior at the table.

Serve breakfast juice in goblets.

Use special silverware for family meals in addition to
Sundays and holidays. (The more you use it, the less you
need to polish it).

Put out the best tablecloths, or use easy-to-wash-and-iron
placemats and runners, especially for small children or
messy meals. Place a tablecloth over a card table, drape it
with a damask runner, and set it on the patio for a surprise
breakfast for two. I know that etiquette books say that you
shouldn't light candles in the daytime or lay placemats over
tablecloths, but I do both. With messy meals like spaghetti, it
is easier to wash a soiled placemat than a tablecloth. Do
whatever is practical for you. There are no etiquette police! I
would rather protect my nice things than go with a lesser-
looking table.

Set the table properly, with style, like this.

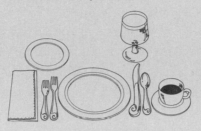

Crystal or silver candlesticks and pedestal serving dishes light up a table; use them for simple, but elegant meals. Use serving dishes instead of putting pots and pans on the table. Or fill everyone's plate in the kitchen before placing on the table.

Cloth napkins folded over bread in a basket keep it warm; used at place settings, they inspire good manners. Make your own from today's easy-wash fabrics, watch for sales, or look for the unusual at antique or thrift stores.

Place a single fresh flower in your most beautiful vase and set it on a breakfast tray for your spouse, a birthday child, or guest. Add a votive candle.

Go for the unusual: float a passion flower in a dish or entwine asparagus fern in ribbon down the center of the table.

Enhance by candlelight: a votive candle at *each* setting, floating candles in bowls, or small candles clustered on mirrors. Center ten white tapers in different crystal holders on a silver tray. Oranges make scrumptuous scented holders (X with a sharp knife at the stem and push in a short taper), also great for banquets. Even simple meals like chili and cornbread are made memorable when eaten by candlelight.

Don't set the table at all! Spread a blanket on the living room floor and have a winter picnic. Put a cloth on the coffee table and eat oriental style sitting on pillows while watching something special on TV. Set up a tent inside and "camp out." Have a progressive dinner with your teens and "progress" from kitchen to dining to patio table with each course.

Make Your Food Appealing

There's food and then there's *food*. Use contrast and balance. Add pizzazz. Learn from the experts by studying cookbooks, magazines, and restaurant ideas.

Drinks

One tea bag of your favorite flavored tea spices up a pitcher of plain iced or sun tea. (I do this all summer.) Add a sprig of mint. Freeze goblets until serving.

A few fresh-squeezed oranges added to your frozen orange juice make it all taste fresh.

Blend one quart of vanilla yogurt with twelve ounces of frozen orange juice; add a few ice cubes (my kids' favorite).

Heated milk, instead of water, makes instant specialty coffees more like special cocoas. Keep gourmet coffee in the freezer for guests.

Arrange tea bags of different kinds in a basket for a choice of flavor.

Main Meals

Offer nutritious food to your family and keep it simple when you're first starting out. Serve the minimim basic four: meat, starch (potatoes, rice, pasta, stuffing), and two side dishes (green and yellow vegetables). Serve fruit with the meal or save for dessert.

Our family loves Italian food. It combines meat and carbohydrate (spaghetti, ravioli, lasagne); we add a green salad and bread. Another favorite is Mexican food which uses grains (corn/wheat) and beans to form protein and complex carbohydrates.

Experiment, or take a class in using spices, herbs, or flavorings. (For example, a stalk or two of celery when boiling chicken for anything will enhance the flavor of the meat.)

For outside dining, inexpensive, oval baskets (like the ones used in the '50s) lined with wax paper make hamburgers fun and easy to clean up. Add fries and a pickle.

When you have the fix-ins for BLT's, add another layer of ham or turkey on toasted bread and make a club. Put in four toothpicks, cut the bread on the diagonal, lay the sandwiches on their sides around the rim—add chips, baked beans, or corn on the cob. Your family will be impressed.

Learn to use a crockpot. Simmer soups, blend stews, boil New England corned beef, and tenderize pot roasts and onions. If you go to work in the morning, prepare everything the night before and place the pot in the refrigerator. Pull it out the next morning and turn it on. When you get home, enjoy the aroma—sit down for a rest!

Side Dishes

Steam several vegetables at once—broccoli stalks, cauliflower, carrots, fresh green beans, squashes, or corn on the cob. Buy what's in season. Choose fresh, then frozen, then canned if nothing else is available.

Appeal to the eye. Cut up raw vegetables: carrot and celery sticks, green and red bell peppers, jicama, cucumbers, Italian squash, turnips. Use pickled beets, Greek wax peppers, black olives, crab apples. All of these make a nice contrast to greens and yellows.

Keep applesauce ready to eat or to top waffles. Sprinkle with cinnamon. Heat it in the winter, chill in summer.

Slice melons of all kinds. Leave the rind on or peel and cut in chunks.

Desserts

When not used as a side dish, finish off a meal with a variety of fresh fruits. Alternate red and green apple slices with orange slices in a circle on a plate; fill in center with sliced bananas, grapes or strawberries. Add fresh pineapple, watermelon, or seasonal berries to ice cream.

Mix eight ounces of softened cream cheese with seven ounces of marshmallow creme for a fruit dip.

Add little extras to common desserts. Drizzle chocolate syrup over bundt cake (no icing). Rum or brandy extract added to puddings puts pizzazz in parfait; top with a stemmed cherry. Use a cup of chocolate chips instead of walnuts in brownies. Add mint or almond flavoring to chocolate cake.

Breakfast

Add sliced tomatoes, cantaloupe, or cottage cheese to a plate of bacon and eggs.

Put raisins, sliced almonds, and brown sugar in oatmeal.

Cut up chunks of chilled melon (cantaloupe, honeydew, canary) and fresh pineapple in a bowl, dollop a scoop of blueberry yogurt or cottage cheese, add seedless grapes, top with granola, raisins, and cashews. (My husband loves this!)

Make basic crepes (two cups flour, two cups milk, four eggs, one-fourth cup oil); cover each with softened cream cheese, fold into fourths, or roll up. Serve with fresh fruit (strawberries, peaches, blueberries) drizzled with honey, cherry pie filling, heated canned spiced apples, flavored syrups, or chocolate syrup with whipped cream and nuts. Store leftover plain crepes in sealed container in refrigerator. Microwave during the week.

School Lunches

Magazines are filled with ideas on improving lunches every fall. Include the main entree, chips or pretzels, fresh fruit, string cheese, something sweet, and 100% juice.

Freeze drink: it will still be cold, but thawed by lunchtime.

When children tire of sandwiches, roll up ham and sliced cheese; fasten with a toothpick. Or use tortillas instead of bread; roll with filling and slice into wheels.

Slice apples and dip in lemon juice to prevent browning. Children are more likely to eat them than a whole apple.

Try not to make lunches a battleground. My children could share or exchange only their dessert or chips with friends. When they needed a change, I packed yogurt, ramen, energy bars, fruit roll-ups, cheese and crackers, and granola bars. If they have access to a microwave, dinner leftovers are great.

. . . . .

Give Your Meals Something Extra

Add some of the following staples to your cabinet or refrigerator to grab for quick entertaining. They give your meals a little panache!

Flavored syrups
Extracts—all flavors
Specialty coffees and teas
Instant cocoa/marshmallows
Frozen lemonade
Cake mixes and frosting
Brownie mixes
Chocolate chips
Nuts of all kinds
Shredded coconut
Marshmallow creme
Cream cheese

Pickles—dill, bread and butter, sweet
Greek wax peppers
Olives—green, black
Pickled okra, spiced beets
Variety of crackers
Hard cheeses—Cheddar, Monterey Jack, and Jalapeno
Diced green chilies
Cans of chili
Variety of salsas
Variety of canned beans
Boxes of rice pilaf
Colored toothpicks

. . . . .

Entertaining

Go the extra mile. Create a beautiful trail of sensory memories not only for your family, but for guests who come and go.

Leave a scented candle burning as a welcome in the guest room. Turn back the blanket and sheet; lay a mint on the pillow. Keep a basket bedside, with simple snacks like granola bars, chewing gum, fresh fruit. Put tissues, magazines, and a clock nearby.

In the bathroom, keep a basket of shampoo and conditioner or lotion samples, extra little towels rolled in a basket, or boxes of paper towels. When little friends visit, paper towels are more hygenic and keep the bathroom tidier.

Make a favorite soft drink or snack available. Offer refreshments when guests arrive—even if unexpected. Walk guests to their car when they leave.

Store child-friendly plates, cups, and silverware for small
guests. A highchair and bibs come in handy, too. I include a
stubby goblet and small knife with their table settings when
children are a little older—kids notice, and it makes them
feel important.

Decorating

Decorate to say "I love you." Making your family comfortable
fits any decor.

Choose the decor you like and buy only styles and colors
that coordinate. Look for one-of-a-kind household items at
craft fairs, thrift shops, or antique markets.

Put candles and potpourri in each bathroom. Aroma is
enhanced in small rooms.

Use live plants throughout your home. They add color and
make everything fresh. Use a variety of holders (wicker baskets, brass, glass, pottery, tin, lucite, terra cotta, silver, lac-
quer). Use things not intended to hold plants like pitchers,
buckets, and copper pots. (Hint: overwatering ruins plants
most often.)

I planted several rose bushes just for cutting blossoms to
bring inside, fragrant jasmine by several windows, and gar-
denia bushes by my front door.

Drape afghans over each chair and sofa for cuddling; also,
lots of pillows make lounging comfortable.

Hang an entire wall of family photos in your hallway for

reminiscing. Children inevitably take their friends there.

Baskets of all shapes and sizes hold seasonal collections or magazines, decorate walls or shelves, carry supplies upstairs, on errands, or to work. Look for bargains to be used as is or to paint.

Buy Creatively for Your Home

Search for items that make daily living interesting and are helpful in entertaining. Purchase . . .

dimestore or discount-house stemware until better can be purchased, and white china that can be dressed up or down by changing the linens (red checks to damask to black and gold).

linens on sale—all sizes, varied colors, lace to denim, for holidays, picnics, etc.

stainless or silverware with a minimum of twelve matching settings, iced-tea spoons, steak knives, and serving pieces.

crystal, silver, or unusual serving pieces that can be used as centerpieces, stored or hung as decorations when not in use (teapots, platters/trays, bowls, candlesticks).

shelves and tables of all types and sizes to display (and store) pretty things.

doilies and lace to use in displaying items.

Teaching Respect Intentionally

Activity:

Have your children draw a line down the middle of a piece of paper, then label one side "Positive Traits" and the other "Negative Traits." Talk about character traits and give the children examples of each. Ask them to name as many as they can think of in five minutes. Read their answers aloud, then challenge them to read Proverbs and write down all the positive traits they can find. (A reward may shorten the time of research.) Help them memorize the positive traits.

Activity:

Buy two similar plants for each of your children. Show them how to water and feed them. Liken the fertilizer to "earned respect," not essential for life, but essential for a fuller, lusher life. In the next few weeks, instruct your child to give one plant only water, the other both water and plant food. Then compare and discuss which is healthier, more robust, or larger. Discuss the law of planting and harvesting.

The Rhythm
of Order

Affection

Respect

Order

Merriment

Affirmation

*D*o what you want as long as you don't hurt anybody!"

"You only live once, so go for all the gusto you can!"

"Look out for ol' Number One!"

These and many more phrases like them are exposing the seductive attitude of this generation who believe they may live without boundaries. "If it feels good, do it!" is a rallying cry for those not wanting to be hemmed in by a list of restrictions. At first it looks and feels good to be free of so-called restraints. A case can be made for such things as "rugged individualism," "a free spirit," or a desire to stretch one's wings. It is true that a person needs freedom to express himself. Many are never loosed from shackles they are unfortunately tied to by past circumstances. To those people, we say, "Break free!" But do so with caution.

On the one extreme, a home that has no rules, where everyone is "a free spirit," is a home in chaos. On the other extreme, a home ruled by an iron fist and negative reinforcement is a home also in chaos. The former is overt chaos manifested openly and visibly, boisterous outwardly. The second, covert chaos, will be quiet outwardly, but will bubble and churn with fear inwardly. In either case, the resulting fragrance will be repulsive, an aroma to which it is not pleasant to come home.

Order
is the act of managing and modeling godly leadership in the home, resulting in a refuge of calm.[1]

Apply the following labels to your own style of parenting:

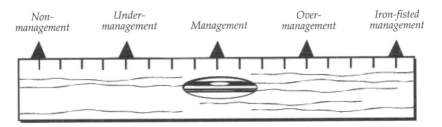

If these words could be placed on a carpenter's level, we suspect the balance bubble would fluctuate back and forth through the middle word *management* at least on a daily, if not an hourly, basis in many homes. Most of us really want to do things right when it comes to this aspect of the family fragrance—*order*. But we sometimes find ourselves in the balancing act of over-and under-management. Which one of the five labels would you most want to be used to describe your parenting style? Which style of parenting did you receive from your mom and dad? Many of us tend to manage the way our parents did, which gives us a tendency to *react* instead of *act* in response to frustration where we feel a lack of parenting skills.

As we attempt to manage our homes and relationships, we must strike a happy balance between two extremes. We don't want liberty to lead to license, or control to lead to confinement.

Our goal is freedom within generous boundaries. The way we manage our homes will be the way our children will manage their world. We are conveying to them—if not in word, at least in deed—how family affairs are to be ordered.

Early in our children's lives, Gail and I were scared to death about the responsibility of parenting. We knew that our every move would be watched and imitated. So we looked for ways of conveying to our children what parenting was teaching us. We realized that the proper conveyance of order would bring security to their world. We tried to treat them the way we would want to be treated. After all, isn't that what Jesus taught? He said, "Do unto others as you would have them do unto you" (Matt.7:12 KJV). That is the ultimate act of conveying order.

We knew our children would meet enough hostile challenges outside the walls of our home, so we wanted them to encounter a place of calm when they came home. The same was true of ourselves as parents. We faced enough negative during the day to know that not much of it was welcome at home. We made a decision together to not allow negative experiences from the outside to be injected into our family fragrance.

An orderly freedom _____

PRINCIPLE: Children need creative freedom within boundaries.

INTENTIONAL IMPACT: To foster a sense of security within the boundaries and rules of our home.

The Johnsons wanted to teach their children the freedom and safety they will experience within secure boundaries. A 6'x 6' square frame was quickly constructed in the middle of the family room. Dad then erected a tent type shelter with a blanket under which the boys and their mom could picnic, watch a video, talk, and laugh. He instructed the children, "as long as you stay within the framework you are safe." He brought a ladder in the house and stood on the top rung along with his weapons (a box of rolled up socks). "When you step out of the boundaries, you may get hit," he said. Across the room on a table, he placed some candy, then dared them to try to get the goodies. When the boys stepped across the boundaries from under the blanket he pelted them with the socks; the boys would head back for cover. Dad was teaching them the security of boundaries and the consequences of breaching them.

When dad descended the ladder, the boys captured the socks and he ran for cover!

After the birth of our first child we realized that calm could not be present without order. Our newborn had to be given an ordered rhythm of sleeping, eating, touching, and loving, or there was no peace. Touching and loving is no problem as new parents, but some find a schedule of eating and sleeping difficult. Gail set the hours for both and usually stuck to them. Our children soon adapted to the order and became happy babies. As they grew, we had to begin to identify their borders: *what* they could touch and *where* they could play. We put valuable items out of reach, but not much else was moved. Our children were taught what a plaything was and was not. Later they were taught to knock before entering private space and not interrupt conversation. As they got older they understood where friends could go in the house. No friend of the opposite sex was allowed in their bedrooms, or for that matter, in the house without one parent present.

All human beings need an understanding of orderly boundaries, and need to know where those boundaries exist. Think of the planets, the moons, the sun, and the stars of our Milky Way. Add a comet darting through. Imagine how chaotic the universe would be without the order of orbits. Beauty would be swallowed up by chaos. Imagine the potential for disaster!

.....

Think of the planets, moon, the sun, and the stars of our Milky Way. Add a comet darting through. Imagine how chaotic the universe would be without the order of orbits; beauty would be swallowed up by chaos!

.....

Watch children on a playground. If there is a fence—a boundary—they will go to the very edge of the playground, even climb on the fence though there may be a busy street just on the other side of it. If there is no fence, watch how the children will tend to huddle near the center of the grounds where it is "safe." When the boundaries aren't clearly defined, children tend to fear uncertainty. The lack of a definitive boundary limits freedom. When a child knows his boundaries, he has complete liberty to go anywhere within those limits. When he is familiar with the boundaries, then creativity can follow.

A home may contain all the ingredients that every home should have—people, nice rooms, furniture, rules, affection, respect—and yet its fragrance becomes odorous when it lacks boundaries. Established order makes children comfortable. Be

sure your children know the rules of your home and are familiar with the consequences of stepping outside those rules. That
knowledge instills within them a sense of security. By honoring
the rules of the home and by encouraging everyone in the
household to live according to them, the atmosphere is set up
for calm.

John Rosemond, psychologist and journalist, whose syndi-
cated column *Parenting* appears in Sunday papers across
America, recently wrote:

This may cause great dismay among parents everywhere,
but it's a fact:

No matter what your child's age, no matter how hard you
try, no matter what disciplinary techniques you use, you
cannot control your child. The only thing you can effectively control is your relationship with your child. In this
regard, there are three kinds of parents.

1. Parents who try to control their children. These parents—
termed authoritarian—are dictatorial and rigidly restric-
tive. Because they are attempting to do the impossible, and
because they do not accept children for what they are,
authoritarian parents are frequently angry and frustrated,
and they almost always overdiscipline, using a hammer
when they could have used a flyswatter.

2. Parents who fail to control their relationships with their
children. These parents are often termed "permissive." I
prefer wimp. They try to be friends with their children, let
their children make decisions they're incapable of making,
try to keep their children happy, compromise and capitulate
in the face of conflict, and are generally at their children's
beck and call.

3. Parents who make no attempt to control their children, but are in complete control of their relationships with their children. These parents are authoritative. They make rules and enforce them dispassionately. They supervise well but are not highly involved with their kids. They describe their own boundaries to their children, thus helping their children learn to stand on their own two feet.

In [the first two categories] we're talking about parents who are ruled by emotion. The authoritarian parent is ruled by frustration and anger, the permissive parent by anxiety and guilt. The authoritative parent, by contrast, rules. He is not in the sway of emotion, but neither is he unemotional.

The authoritative parent, for example, realizes that (a) while he cannot make a four-year-old share toys with playmates, he can confiscate those toys the youngster refuses to share; (b) while he cannot prevent a ten-year-old from misbehaving in school, he can revoke privileges at home; and (c) he can't make a teenager get good grades, but can refuse to let the youngster get a driver's license until grades improve.

He also knows that regardless of what he does, the child in question may not change his or her behavior. He is simply resolved to teach the child that choices result in consequences.[2]

In whatever management style you may find yourself, let us encourage you not to give up. Find a place of moderation. The basis for achieving freedom and harmony in the home is through creating orderly rhythm in daily rituals and habits.

Until the twentieth century, daily life was regulated by nature—work and play had to be done during the daylight, and people rested during the night. But the Industrial Revolution of the nineteenth century changed all that. Modern progress made it possible for business and families to overcome the limitations of nature—we now enjoy plums, peaches, and grapes imported from South America in the middle of winter, and stay up all night working on a car, a craft, or a portfolio because of electricity. But just because it is possible, doesn't mean we necessarily benefit from breaking natural rhythms.

As teachers, Gail and I have observed tired teens and whiny kindergartners—perhaps because they habitually stay up too late. As parents we have seen the hysteria of TV sports and the local illuminated field sap the focus of many families. But for what ultimate purpose? We are not against any of these things—the Super Bowl, World Series, T-Ball, Little League, or the soccer season—but much of the frenzy of modern life has been brought about because of the availability of too many activities.

As adults who came of age in the '60s, Gail and I see ourselves surrounded by the aftermath of society's revolution. Being in but not necessarily of the upwardly mobile yuppie era, we find we usually have more in common with the more structured and less materialistic World War II generation. That disciplined majority seemed to have fewer *things* but more *time* to share with their families. The distinctions between wrong and right and black and white were not so blurred. Since we're about to come to the end of the twentieth century, we agree with others that it's time for "the '60s" to be over. Moving forward to restore order and rhythm to family life, we believe that the peace Christ offers us to enjoy is the answer.

We all have to make choices to give up good things for better things, career advancement for family enhancement, temporary things for eternal values. We're not against striving to be the best at what you do, but with families there is much at stake. The next generation, bringing in the twenty-first century, is too important.

An atmosphere that brings calm _____

PRINCIPLE: We are to become imitators of the heart of Christ.

INTENTIONAL IMPACT: To lead our child to find his own answers and encounter truth for himself.

The Chandler family loaded the kids into the car to head for the amusement park in a big city near their home. Hardly twenty minutes into the trip, an argument ensued between the two siblings in the back seat. One had brought a book that the other wanted to see. He said, "No" and, well, you know what followed.

The initial impulse of the mother was to turn the car around, but that would only have added to the problem. It certainly would not have solved anything. Instead of trying to figure out who was right or wrong, and instead of threatening the kids, Mom decided to help the kids find their own answer. "I'm going to watch you both and find out who is going to be the best example of unselfishness. I think at least one of you knows how to be a good example."

Silence!

One brother gave the book up to the other. The recipient held it up with a sheepish look on his face. After seeing his brother praised for his

unselfish attitude, he in turn tried to "out-unselfish" his brother's
good deed by returning the book and offering to share his other toys.

The Scriptures tell the story of two mothers who went before King Solomon, each claiming a certain baby as her own. In reality, one woman's baby had been accidentally killed, and she had stolen the other's baby. Solomon did not beat the truth out of the women, nor did he give them a sophisticated polygraph. The wise king simply created an atmosphere for the truth to emerge through the arguing parties themselves. In the same way the Chandler brothers found the answer to their own problem when an atmosphere was created to allow selfishness to change.

. . . . .

Children are endowed with a desire to please and belong, which gives parents a perfect avenue to teach.

. . . . .

Gail and I didn't ascribe to the dictum "Listen to what I say." We followed as close as possible "Listen to what I *do* as I follow Christ." Isn't it true that our children do not have to be instructed in the way of selfishness? It just comes with human nature. No child is exempt. But children are endowed with a desire to please and belong which gives parents a perfect avenue to teach. By tapping into their soft hearts and praising them for showing positive traits (like telling the truth, sharing, and respecting others and others' possessions), parents begin to create an atmosphere for truth to emerge.

My secretary told me of an incident where her six year old was accused of squeezing red punch on the front door of a neighbor's house. When the neighbor asked them about it, Sherry didn't think her son was guilty, but the neighbor told her

the boy had owned up to it. When she and her husband confronted Kory, he confirmed his involvement and promptly made
restitution by cleaning it off. I was struck by the way he didn't lie
about it even though that would have been easy. A time of teaching followed. "Hurting others' property isn't acceptable" he was
told, but neither was he left with a negative reprimand. He was
praised for telling the truth. He is being raised in an atmosphere
where truth is important, and his soft heart responds.

The Fragrance of Order—Guidelines

1. Make rules that can be kept.

Maybe a better way to say this is "Make rules that make sense."
Rules that make no sense because they cannot be kept are either
unenforceable, or fierce battlegrounds. Evaluate the rules of the
house and eliminate those that are not necessary. Flexibility and
creative alternatives will help avoid future head-butting. For
instance, if your child has decided to take piano lessons, you
may require her to practice a half hour each day. But there are
days that a half hour of practice won't be possible, so doesn't it
make more sense to say three hours a week? Those three hours
may be divided with flexibility. That gives your child a day off
occasionally in case something else fun comes up.

When our children took music lessons, we asked them to
practice thirty minutes a day. But thirty minutes seemed like
forever to them (and to us!). So we let them divide it into ten-
minute increments: before school, when they got home, and in
the evening. We actually got more and better practice from
them.

2. Hold periodic family meetings to enable clear communication about order.

Rules are subject to private interpretation. Left to themselves, people will interpret anything according to their own perspectives. Clarification is necessary, and family meetings help alleviate intentional or accidental misunderstandings. But they should not turn into open forums for bellyaching. They should serve to unify. Some families call "stand-up" meetings. Others incorporate them into their evening meal or just afterwards. In the Brooks' two-story home there is a balcony that overlooks the family room. Dad and Mom will invite the children to the balcony where they will discuss and coordinate everyone's plans for the day, or clarify the reason why a daughter's boyfriend isn't allowed to go to her room to listen to a CD.

> *Where and when is the best time for your family to get together? Wherever and whenever it works best for your family. But if you don't intentionally plan, it won't "just happen."*

Where and when is the best time for your family to get together? Wherever and whenever it works best for *your* family. But if you don't intentionally plan, it won't "just happen."

3. For younger children, frequent distraction is more beneficial than punishment.

Of course, order includes discipline and its consequences. But with younger children, less discipline will be needed if the distraction level can be increased. Due to their short attention span, this tactic is a clever way to lower the number of confrontations, thus allowing you to heighten morale in the family.

One common place of confrontation is the grocery checkout stand where the candy rack screams for attention. Folks, that "ain't by accident." So be prepared to distract. Bring something in your handbag that you can pull out at the critical moment. When you eat out with your children, keep toys in a bag prepared ahead of time. Can adults really expect children to sit still as long as we? The reason they act childish is because they are children. When they begin to get restless, produce fun things with which they don't normally play like a suction toy to stick on their highchair tray, a favorite coloring book and crayons, or a special picture book that you have saved for these occasions.

4. Develop your personal family rhythm and follow it.

Infants and small children need regular nap, bedtime, and even Sunday schedules. Older children will need regular reading and prayer time, family night activities, and sport or music practice. Teens need to have church youth activities and social times at friends' houses, and eventually even dating scheduled into the family calender. Your family's rhythm will change periodically as new members are added or as children mature. Be flexible. Be willing to change with the years.

Our friends Lisa and Tom Rasmussen did a great job as their two boys became teenagers. After-school activities, practices, and jobs made it difficult to get together for dinner as had been their tradition. Lisa and Tom began getting up earlier every morning and sharing a big breakfast with their sons. They read the Scriptures together, shared stories, and went over their daily schedules. Rarely were they all together again until the next morning. What an impact this made on all of them, but especially on the boys as they began to leave home! (One son is now married and has a little one of his own; they still get together at Mom and Dad's on Saturday mornings for breakfast—because they want to.)

5. Order, internalized, brings outward peace.

We want order to become a part of children's lives, because it will bring with it a calm to the home and a peaceful heart that will later extend out toward others. The Bible says, "the steps of a good man are ordered by the Lord" (Ps. 37:23 NKJV). Basically that means the good man is listening to his Lord, knows what is expected, and follows it. Knowing what is expected of them brings a sense of security to children not unlike the feeling of traveling a familiar path. Our children need to know what we expect before they are able to fol-low, generous freedom within set limits, and parents who model order and calm.

Etiquette is really just a structured way of letting people know you care about them.

When a child catches on to how order relieves outward chaos, he will internalize it and make use of it. Gail and I saw this take root in our children's lives. We taught our children to set out the clothes and shoes that they were to wear to school the next day. (This should include lunch bag and school book bag.) When they did, it closed down a potential area of conflict the next morning. Also, each of our childen had specific chores. They came home and immediately tackled homework, chores, and music practice. When the work wasn't done satisfactorily, only one child was confronted, not the entire clan. There was no arguing to find out who was responsible and who didn't do his job. With jobs out of the way, the children created their own freedom for the remainder of the day. They let their friends know that was the rhythm of things in their lives, and everyone adjusted. Some of their friends saw the benefits of it and followed suit, knowing that our children wouldn't emerge for play until first things were done first.

Fragrant Tips from Gail

When we hear the word *order*, it may conjure up in our minds someone who is barking orders at us or telling us how bad we are being, wagging their pointer finger in our faces. But let the word take on a new meaning of peace, rhythm, and a lack of friction. How would a band sound without rhythm or beat, each player just deciding to "do his own thing"? At the next concert you hear, listen to the warm-up. Even though everyone looks impressive, dresses stylishly, and embraces wonderful musical instruments, the sound will be chaotic, won't it? When your heartbeat is not in rhythm, you have a serious problem. When some system in your body becomes "out of order," we say it is diseased or dysfunctional. To keep things running smoothly, families need order, too.

Mealtimes

Good manners are similiar to good grammar—neither stands out except when they are lacking on the one extreme or pretentious on the other. Etiquette is really just a structured way of letting people know you care about them. You may notice that a lot of *order* focuses around mealtimes because the dinner table is the parents' primary classroom.

Here are the expectations we held in our family and required our children to respect:

Come home to dinner on time, or call.

Come to the table cleaned up, with hands washed.

Boys and girls help set the table, and do it right.
At our Christian high school, I teach a class on etiquette, and the section ends with a very fancy candlelight dinner. The class members supply all the food for the four-course meal, and contribute many of the decorations. We use white linen, silver, crystal—the works. Every student is responsible to bring his own place setting of fine china, two goblets, silverware, and a cloth napkin. The variety of china place settings really adds to the beauty of the table. I set the chairs in place, and assign place cards. Each student then has to prepare his own place at the table without help, including proper placement of the folded napkin and the teacup handle at "three o'clock."

My older children and many of their friends have taken the class, and when they eat in our home, they volunteer to set the table, or check to see that it's done right! (When our son, Matthew, had to give a demonstration speech his freshmen year of college, he demonstrated how to properly set a table. His class loved it and the prof gave him an "A".)

Children are encouraged to decorate the table, arrange the candles, and make a centerpiece.

Come to the table immediately when called to eat. (This issue can be a real pet peeve to moms. It isn't easy to prepare a meal and have it all finished at the same time. If she has to prod and beg everyone to leave their computer, TV, basket-ball game, or phone conversation, it can be discouraging. Dad may have to step in to see that Mom's efforts are honored if this becomes a problem.)

Leave lids on casseroles and cover all hot food until after prayer. When removed, have someone take them to the kitchen counter.

Hold hands during prayer. This gives comradery and keeps little ones' hands occupied while everyone's eyes are closed. You may allow the children to take turns praying; their prayers aren't always conventional, and I'm sure they make God smile. They make great memories, too.

Pass the food to the right. Each person should take whatever is on the table in front of his plate, serve himself, and then pass it to the next person. When it comes back around to him, he can put it back in the center of the table. And if it is a favorite food item, a child can be taught to look around and see if everyone has been served—discreetly—before he decides to take super-sized helpings of any food.

Do not answer the phone during mealtime: let the machine take the call! Show children you cherish time with them. And Mom appreciates not letting her efforts get cold while someone is away from the table on the phone. (You may want to screen the call to be sure it is not an emergency, but it rarely is. Call back later. Children's friends quickly catch on.)

Pick up used dinner plates before serving dessert on a small plate with a fresh fork.

After dinner, when adults linger, excuse children from the table. A child can ask, "May I be excused from the table?" if he needs to exit early.

Clean up is easier if everyone automatically carries his own dishes to the kitchen. Silverware may be sorted into slots in the dishwasher for easy unloading. Hand wash crystal goblets, dry, and put away as soon as possible after a meal; they quickly become cloudy if washed in the dishwasher, and if left on the counter are easy to bump over and break. You may want to hand wash sterling silverware, too, though I do know people who clean it in the dishwasher with good results. I always soak mine in soapy hot water while we clear the table, then wash it by hand.

Modesty Revisited

When you teach children in the home to have good manners, to be disciplined, to think before speaking, to be gracious, and other life lessons, it carries over into other relationships. Now our family has a lot of inside jokes and what we call "family talk." Anyone who knows J. Otis and me certainly wouldn't associate us with the word "prude," but we do believe Americans have gone overboard in doing what is natural and "letting it all hang out." People have lost a lot of natural inhibitions. You may want to consider getting your family reacquainted with words like *blush, deference, modesty, feminine, masculine,* and other words that seem out of date. You may want to reestablish that some things are not appropriate in mixed company, that young adults are expected to act like ladies and gentlemen. Where can we depend on important values being intentionally taught? In our homes.

A lack of modesty shows a lack of respect. Do a word study on the meaning of "unseemly" in 1 Corinthians 13:5

(KJV), and "nakedness" in Leviticus 18 and 20, especially in the NKJV. Common sense teaches us that if we flaunt the forbidden, we needn't be surprised when the scandalous happens. In our sex-crazed world, how can we balance what is normal, and give sex its place of beauty and dignity in our homes without being priggish? And how can we protect our male children particularly, who have a stronger sex drive, from being preoccupied with sex? In this day of the unthinkable and the abusive, we have to teach our children to respect their bodies and the bodies of others. The old dictum, "An ounce of prevention is worth a pound of cure" is certainly true. We

> *People have lost a lot of natural inhibitions. You may want to consider getting the family reacquainted with words like blush, deference, modesty, feminine, masculine, and other words that seem out of date.*

want to prevent as much "baggage" being carried into our children's adult lives as possible, and the home is the ideal place to learn appropriateness. God forbids parents to go about in a state of undress in front of their children. Consider some of these ideas used by parents who have been able to raise sexually healthy adolescents:

If a bedroom or bathroom door is closed or mostly closed, children need to knock and wait for a response before entering.

Children should knock on the hall wall before entering their parents' bedroom if the door is open. They should not bring their friends into their parents' room or bath even when the room is not occupied. Private rooms are just that—private.

Friends of the opposite sex are not allowed in bedrooms. This one hard and fast rule eliminates many potential problems. When our children had friends overnight on the same night, once the girls' door was closed, it was closed for the night. The guys often slept in the living room—by the kitchen— where they had more room. J. Otis and I also left our door wide open, just to be sure. We didn't announce these rules at the beginning of each evening, nor did we suggest, even in jest, that we were on the lookout for anything suspicious. Our children shared these rules with their friends.

Don't allow family members to lounge around in their underwear once they have come close to the age of puberty—especially prudent when there are teens of the opposite sex in the home. Girls need to have a simple robe to throw on to dash back and forth to the bathroom even if wearing a bra and panties. Boys walking about in outer shorts is perfectly acceptable, however.

Close the door when using the toilet. Although this seems like such a "no-brainer," our children have gone into homes of good people who never close the bathroom door for anything. It made them uncomfortable and hesitant about visiting again.

What about swimming in this day of the bikini, the thong, the Speedo, and when Europe goes topless? There's not much we can do about the rest of the world, but our family can't participate in those kinds of activities and not expect to run into trouble.

Once the children were adolescents, we bought them stylish, but the least-revealing swimsuits we could find. Some years were easier than others. We allowed them to go swimming with friends only if we knew who else was going to be there. A few times, our girls had "other plans" if we weren't comfortable with the young men who would be present. Call us old-fashioned, but we have never felt obliged to let our daughters be ogled by presumptuous young men; once swimming was over, they did not lounge around in their suits, but put on a wrap or cover-up. Our older two watched out for each other.

This may vary greatly from family to family, and each must decide for itself. We are a very "touchy, feely" family. We have a close relationship with our teens, and even when they may have rolled their eyes at some of our stipulations, they knew we loved them more than anything and were looking out for their best interests.

Bedtimes

We've talked before about the pleasures of putting our children to bed and waking them up, but we need to look at some ideas on the rhythm of the rituals themselves. Make bedtime a fun, relaxing ritual. Get into a routine. Since we no longer go to bed when the sun goes down, how might we get them from activity to "lights out" calmly?

Give small children a warning. "It's almost time for bed," before you want them to get ready instead of stopping them abruptly. A little later say, "Okay, it's time to put the toys away and get ready for bed."

Help them put away their toys instead of expecting them to do it by themselves. If you leave them, they will get distracted and get interested in another toy!

Parents may choose to split bedtime chores. Maybe Dad wants to be in charge of baths and Mom take care of reading, or visa versa. Or maybe this can be solely Dad's area of quality time. Do whatever works best for your family.

When Matt and Becky were infants, I disliked all the mess of portable bathtubs. I was small and it was a little awkward. I began handing them in to J. Otis when he was in the shower. Some men may not feel too safe holding these slippery bundles, but he was a piano player and had very strong hands. He began to look forward to it, and would sing and play with them while he washed them up. He always handed me back a laughing baby. That little ritual probably saved me hours during their first year. (Sometimes when I was in the shower, he even handed them to me.) When they were older and able to sit up in one of those bath seat contraptions, I moved them to the regular tub.

An older child may enjoy reading to younger siblings. Whenever our children volunteered, we let them. It was good for all of us.

We wanted our children to be able to sleep in any situation and did not want them to need nightlights in their rooms. Lights can easily become a habit. Unless they went through a time of being a light sleeper, we left their doors partly open. We wanted them to get use to house noises because we had people over frequently, and J. Otis played and wrote music whenever he got an idea. If children associate bedtime with contentment, relaxation, and a loving adult, these comforting rhythms will allow them to sleep anywhere, anytime, anyplace. They will happily stay at Grandma's or at home with a sitter and give you a break. The rituals give them security. If someone needed total quiet to be able to go to sleep, we would all have been in trouble. Our children got used to a "family buzz," and even found it comforting.

Times of Vulnerability

Teaching for over twenty-five years has shown me that we are fearful people. But God wants us unafraid. I have observed that children's unnatural fears are usually passed down in families. Take conscious steps to get over your own fears so you won't pass them to your children. Many childhood fears result from *lack* of security—lack of preparation, ritual, or family rhythm. I'm not talking about terror that comes from abuse and dysfunction, but fears that result accidentally by well-meaning parents. Of course, children should be taught to fear some things like traffic, deep water, and the stove. But I'm talking about unwarranted fears like darkness, howling wind, cats and dogs, or things that go bump in the night. Parents first need to see fears for what they are—not reality.

If your children are afraid of the darkness, take them out in the backyard on a moonless night, and lie on your backs in the grass. Talk about all the good things that happen because of darkness—rest, sleep, starlight. Name some of the industries that go on during the night such as bakeries, dairies, newspapers, and police patrols protecting us. A little understanding may alleviate much of their fear.

The Cavazos family uses a spray bottle filled with water

as "disappearing potion." When their kids are afraid to walk into a dark room for fear of what might lurk there, a spray of the potion clears the way. The power is in their hands, and freedom from fear is just a spray away.

Many children are petrified by storms and not surprisingly, I have found their adult family members usually are, too. Teach caution concerning inclimate weather, but encourage children to enjoy God's variety. I was raised in Michigan where we had wonderful thunderstorms with crashing lightning. Here in California, rain is only seasonal, and real storms are rare. For years, I opened every door and window protected by a porch or awning when it rained, just for the joy of it. Today, none of our children are afraid of thunderstorms in California at least—they think they're a treat!

Church

Before the '60s, society's rules were more structured. We all had two wardrobes: our regular clothes and Sunday Best. We dressed up for church, going downtown, going out on the town, and going to the doctor. Children were not allowed to talk in church or in town meetings. We weren't such a child-centered society as we are today. Newer parents haven't been taught skills to help children behave in any kind of meeting where there is a speaker. If we are serious about good behavior, children need to know we will enforce order. Otherwise, church will become a battleground of wills—or worse for everyone involved, the parents will quit going until the child "is older."

With a little one, sit near the back or near an exit. Prepare him for what is going to take place ahead of time. Tell him he may only whisper in your ear once the preaching begins, and then only to ask questions.

Bring a "Sunday only" bag filled with quiet activities: crayons and a coloring book, a good picture book, etc. No jingling keys or anything that will disturb others. Our older children had a special bag through lower elementary. They listened to what the preacher was saying and easily discussed the sermon afterwards. The activity kept them from being bored.

For several years, Mrs. Cook, my "Other Mother," brought a special "Sunday bag" for our Leah who sat with her and her husband during the Sunday morning service. Mrs. Cook took care in what was placed in the bag, and always had a treat for Leah after church. Leah was never allowed to take the bag home, and was always on her best behavior. When Leah grew up and began to sit with friends, it was rather sad for both Mrs. Cook and me. She carried Leah's bag for several weeks to make sure that phase really was over. Today Leah never leaves church without giving Mrs. Cook a hug.

Don't "shshh" your children when you want them to be quiet—that just makes more noise. Sit between siblings if they talk. If they insist on disturbing—and all kids do at least once—give them a consequence and carry through on it; don't keep threatening over and over. There are differences in personality, but taking action is effective for every child. Children respond to action, not threats. J. Otis says, "It took an arched eyebrow from my mother to know that I was in trouble, and that my behavior had better correct itself pronto."

Joy, Matt's wife, relates this anecdote: "One Sunday I

sat near a little pre-school girl who began to make quite a stir. Her parents kept shshhing her and gave her repeated warnings. She began to cry, and they kept threatening to take her out. To everyone's relief, they finally did. Right when they got to the door, she turned to the audience and pitifully said, 'Help!' Everyone laughed, and the pastor said something funny to relieve the charged atmosphere. This child was a master at manipulating her parents."

My sister and I were trusted enough to sit with our friends from the time we were in junior high. As with other discipline, we weren't punished for carelessness or forgetfulness, but we were in trouble for defiance . . . and it happened once. The punishment was the dreaded "Scarlet Front Row" for us, since Dad, of course, was on the platform and Mom sang in the choir. I felt like I had a huge red "T" on my chest for Talker.
Matt

Oh yes, the front row punishment! Our parents didn't glare at us or act like anything was unusual, but it was pretty obvious to the congregation why we were sitting center front. We had been warned about fooling around with our friends in church, but like every teen, we thought we could live on the edge. Our parents were pretty matter-of-fact; there would be no changing their minds. Matt and I decided to make the best of it, and we did—for two months of Sundays, then they gave us time off for good behavior! All they would have to do is mention the front row again to make us straighten up. We knew they meant it.
Becky

Don't allow your children to leave a service of one to one-and- a-half hours to go to the bathroom or get a drink. Children usually play longer than that. Get them into the habit of making sure they go ahead of time. But if they forget, and don't have a physical problem, let them sit there and be uncomfortable—it usually only happens once. They will go through all kinds of contortions to try to break you. But if you give in, you will only have to go through the same situation again and again. We are not talking about emergencies. Children who become "aisle athletes" frequently do so just to get attention—and because we allow it.

❖Chapter 5❖

Fun Anyone?—
Merriment

Affection

Respect

Order

Merriment

Affirmation

*L*aughter and enthusiasm are the glue that make the other four elements of family fragrance stick together. Without merriment, family life is staid and stale. Most parents are all too familiar with the downward spiral family morale can take. It usually begins with an ungrateful spirit or an attitude of unthankfulness somewhere, and will drive any parent to the brink of insanity. But just as certain steps lead to the downward spiral, certain steps will create an upward spiral.

Because merriment is so important to me, I set out to have a blast with our children from the beginning of their lives. When they were little, I tried to pull the wool over their eyes just to create fun and giggles in our home. Playing hide-and-seek with Matthew when he was about twenty months old brought a lot of that. I would hide in the entryway closet every time—and he knew it. So he would come to the closet door, knock, and ask in his inquisitive little voice, "Daddy, you in there?"

"No," I would answer, "I'm in the bedroom."

"Oh," he would say, and take off for the bedroom. In a minute or two he would return and say, "No, you not."

Rebecca and I loved to drink soft drinks together. My drink would always disappear faster than hers, and hers would never be completely consumed. When she was about two years old, I would get her to look away for a second; then I'd switch cola cans or cups with her. When she turned around, she had the empty cup and I had the full one. When she realized her cup was empty, her first response was only a slight whimper. Then I would say, "What's the matter, hon, is your soda all gone? Here, I'll share some of mine," and would pour half of "my" cup into hers. She was totally satisfied. As she got older, she caught on and would try it on me.

It is this process of the upward spiral that leaves a sweet aroma in the memory of each family member. It all begins with *affection*. An authentically affectionate atmosphere will foster *respect*. When respect has reached full bloom, it facilitates rhythmic *order* in the home. When the first three ingredients are mixed well, the obvious manifestation will be *merriment*.

Merriment
is an atmosphere of enthusiasm
coupled with uninhibited laughter and noise.[1]

Have you ever walked into a home and immediately sensed the fun with which it is filled before anyone said a word? An animated household becomes interesting and infectious to all who live in it and all who visit. Think about it: Merriment is the opposite of boredom. Ardor is the opposite of apathy. Of course, there are times when it is next to impossible to get the morale of the family up. There are times when the dailiness of life brings its own boredom. Don't despair if you find your home that way at times. A fragrant home in which you are living intentionally won't stay down very long!

> *I set out to have a blast with our children from the very beginning of their lives!*

The Cortez family shared how they created a "pick-me-up" during such down times. First, Dad took an old cookie jar to his work bench and repainted it with animated cartoon characters. It read, "Paper Cookies." Then the family got together and listed thirty activities they enjoyed doing together. They folded them like fortune cookies, numbered them according to the cost and time involved, mixed them up, and placed them in the jar. Number one—the best activity—might say, "Everyone take the day off and go to the beach!" Number thirty might read, "Order pizza and rent a movie." Everyone had many ideas to add to the jar. Whenever spirits were low, the family would gather around the jar to draw out a paper cookie. The kids loved the anticipation. A cheer would go up and the whole family would set about doing whatever was written on the paper. Dad always liked to pull out the "cookie" and create on-purpose delays while reading it. Most of the time he would be mobbed if he delayed too long. The stipulation was that the paper cookie jar could only be used once in each month; otherwise it would lose its charm.

A jolly good dose of mirth _____

PRINCIPLE: Learn abundant-life living as a family.

INTENTIONAL IMPACT: To produce in our home abundant-life living that creates freedom and inspires liveliness and enthusiasm.

If anyone ever had a right to shoot down the principle of "abundant-life living," it would be seventy-year-old Joann Anders. Her life seemed to be a recipe for pain. At the age of five she was striken with polio. Her father could not bear the fact that his daughter might never walk, so he left her to be raised by her godly grandfather.

. . . . .

An animated household becomes interesting and infectious to all who live in it and all who visit.

. . . . .

"I remember one day my father promised to visit me in the hospital," she said. "I was so excited. I sat by the window every day for two weeks watching for him to appear. He never came, then or ever." Later, she was abandoned by her mate in midlife, and left with three children to raise.

Yes, there have been very dark moments, but you wouldn't know it. Joann has chosen not to dwell on those. Joy is all over her. When she rolls her wheelchair to the front of the sanctuary on Sunday mornings, I say to myself, "There is a picture of life abundant."

This past Christmas Joann wrote to me, "I hadn't realized I had moved to life's stage where the best was yet to come.' How joyful it has been to learn that!"

J. Otis

. . . . .

There is life after failure. Each hard thing we go through becomes an opportunity— whether we gain or lose by it— that just adds more value to our existence.

. . . . .

Life was created by God with the intention that it be enjoyed. Sin interdicted that plan. Jesus came to restore it, but the plan of salvation goes farther than merely enjoying life. Jesus came to bring abundant life (John 10:10 KJV), something superior to the former, because it assumes joy is possible and viable even in the midst of less-than-perfect circumstances. Even when sin— our own, or someone else's— messes up our dreams.

There is life after failure. There is life after losing. Even our own personal testings are given to enhance life, to make it worth more when we finally overcome each trial. Joseph explained this principle to his brothers when defusing the explosiveness of a seemingly bad family issue. "You meant evil against me;" he said to them, "but God meant it for good, in order to bring it about as it is this day, to save many people alive" (Gen. 50:20 NKJV). Each hard thing we go through becomes an opportunity—whether we gain or lose by it—that just adds more value to our existence. For Joseph, being dumped by his brothers meant a life that would ultimately save his nation. What might it be for you? This verse: "Now to Him who is able to do exceedingly *abundantly* above all that we ask or think, according to the power that works in us" (Eph. 3:20 NKJV) is not a recipe for a sorrowful, poor-old-me style of life. In my opinion, this sounds like freedom to live with merriment no matter who, or what, brings us down.

The level of merriment or liveliness manifested in the home will identify the level of freedom in the family to do a little creative bonding. When our children were busy having fun, their young minds would come up with new ideas for games that sometimes made absolutely no sense to us as adults, but were hilarious. Other times we all developed games together. Family baseball has become one of our favorite activities on holidays, when weather permits. It started out with Mom and Matt against Becky and me, and has evolved to include new family members, in-laws, and grandparents. We have our own set of rules that fit the pace and flow of the game so that the playing field is level. We use only three bases: home, first, and second make a perfect triangle. In order to throw someone out, we simply have to toss the ball—it may be a tennis ball, whiffle ball, or foam ball—between the runner and the base or place a throw toward the runner from the outfield. This way, the little ones aren't forced to catch a hard-thrown ball.

One day, Grandma Hover was talked into playing. By the luck of the draw, I got Grandma for my pitcher. She can't throw a ball within twenty feet of the plate. In fact, one of her pitches intended for the plate flew back over her head and landed where second base usually rests. I looked like an octopus falling out of a tree flailing the bat, running around home plate just to get near a pitch. I never once made contact with the ball in that game. The kids loved it! They still laugh about the awkwardness of my swing, and remind me of what a liability I am to a team. Not to worry, though; someday they'll draw Grandma for a pitcher!

We have been amazed at how animated our kids could become when they entered in on the joking and laughing, much of it directed at Dad. They love to get me when I'm not paying close attention to the flow of activities, or when misfortune falls my way. If you walked in on a family night or on Sunday dinner at our house, you might get the impression that our home is chaotic. Not so! There is meaning and method to all of it. The liveliness and animation create a cheerful atmosphere, a rhythmic purposeful noise, blending into a redolent fragrance. I believe this is what the Psalmist David is explaining in Psalm 68. Listen to his encouragement to family fun: "But let the righteous be glad; Let them rejoice before God; Yes, let them rejoice exceedingly. Sing to God, sing praises to His name; Extol Him who rides on the clouds . . . And rejoice before Him. A father of the fatherless, a defender of widows, [and I believe this includes the single moms] . . . God sets the solitary in families, He brings out those who are bound into prosperity . . ." (Ps. 68:3-6 NKJV).

> *. . . . .*
>
> *I looked like an octopus falling out of a tree flailing the bat. The kids loved it!*
>
> *. . . . .*

The memory of fun will help all family members overcome the times that will seem hard. We'll be reminded that a better time can be just around the corner, no matter the circumstance.

Laughter: an easy pill to swallow _____

PRINCIPLE: Laughter does good like a medicine to every member of the family.

INTENTIONAL IMPACT: To teach our children that life is important, but they must never take it so seriously that laughter and merriment are omitted.

Last summer, the temperature here in Fresno soared to over 110 degrees. The power went out all over town; we were notified it would remain out for hours. The house was sweltering. The married kids all live in the same apartment complex, and their power went out, too. They thought it would be cooler at our house, so they all came over. Irritability could easily have set in. Instead we all grabbed blankets and headed outside for the shade around supper time. We lay down on the blankets and told stories. A potentially irritating situation where nerves are exposed turned into a time of sidesplitting laughter. We brought up some of our most embarrassing moments, remembered past happenings, laughed at things like Grandma and family baseball, giggled into our iced tea, and later smiled while marveling at the beauty of the night sky. Since then, when the weather begins to turn hot, we talk about that night and laugh some more.

Gail

Life does come with a serious side. One needs only a little experience to realize the truth of Job's words, that life "is of few days and full of trouble" (Job 14:1 NKJV). There are times, when feelings are sensitive and nerves raw, that gaiety and joking may be out of order. But usually when a negative emotion overwhelms someone or threatens to consume a family, things won't seem so bad if you take the time to laugh at yourselves. In fact, a good laugh will perk up your spirits and make you, and everyone around you, feel downright refreshed. Whether pain comes in physical or emotional form, it is okay to have an anesthesia, and often a shot of laughter can take the edge off the hurt. Later, the pain can be remembered as an exam that Professor Life administered in his classroom.

One only has to observe how the father of the prodigal

ended the pain of his son (Luke 15:22-24). The family didn't take off two weeks to mourn. Dad must have known the healing power of merriment because he threw a huge party with dancing, noise, eating, music, and, I believe, a good amount of laughter. He knew his son needed to look at himself from the outside as a forgiven person. Nothing else mattered at that moment.

C.S. Lewis said that "humor involves a sense of proportion, and a power of seeing yourself from the outside."[2] Lessons learned, laughter returns.

The Fragrance of Merriment—Guidelines

1. Learn to laugh at yourself.

Laughing at yourself when things go wrong will teach your children that it is okay to not take life's curve balls to heart. It shows you believe everyone will get another chance to step up to the plate to take a better swing. Being self-effacive can also raise your level of acceptance by others most of the time. It is a type of submission, because others can see that you don't take yourself too seriously, and begin to view you as approachable.

I am reminded of the first time I stepped to the plate to face my brother-in-law's fast pitch in a softball game. He was known in the city league as one of the best pitchers. His fastball was almost legendary. I was sure I could hit it, although to be honest, I was a little afraid. I knew if it hit me, it was curtains. Bill also possessed a pitch that spun and looked like a fastball, but was actually a slow curve. When he threw that one I was sure I was going to be hit, so I bailed out of the batter's box as the ball slowly curved over the plate. Everyone was amused, but I was relieved! I looked over to the dugout and laughed with everyone else—hysterically.

Sometimes life does that, too. We will get a curve instead of a fastball. We dodge or bail out. A little laughter takes the edge off when you look around to those who observed. A big grin signals you are OK. Then step back to the plate! Life goes on.

2. Laughter must always be with and not at someone.

There are times when someone has wallowed in the circumstance too long. When the wallowing presents potential danger of deepening, a little laughter or well-placed joking can lift them up. But enter that space carefully. Pointed, purposeful, and hurtful sarcasm should not find its way into your home. Laughter can relieve pain, but used in a wrong way can also cause pain. Laughing *with* someone means that they have seen the humor of a situation themselves. Laughing *at* someone means that they have yet to come to grips with the circumstance.

. . . . .

One only has to observe how the father of the prodigal ended the pain of his son. He must have known the healing power of merriment because he threw a huge party with dancing, noise, eating, music, and I believe, a good amount of laughter.

. . . . .

3. Liveliness and laughter have boundaries.

There will come a moment when it is time to let go of teasing over some circumstance. We have all heard people say "OK, it's not funny anymore." Before that moment comes, drop it. When Jerry broke up with his girlfriend for another girl, Mike just could not let the teasing go. Jerry indicated on several occasions that it was time to end it. Mike called him "dreamer" once too often, and in a public social gathering, a scuffle ensued. Both lost face and respect.

. . . . .

Sometimes life does that . . . we get a curve instead of a fastball. We dodge or bail out. A big grin to the infield signals you are OK.

. . . . .

Be discerning and sensitive to what others may be feeling, especially children, before it becomes embarrassing to them and yourself. Look for signs in their body language and in their eyes. Listen for hints they may drop your direction. When you sense it, back off.

Freedom that inspires merriment doesn't include vulgar fun either. The sacred needs to be kept sacred. Personal matters should be kept private. Poking inappropriate fun at those in a place of authority in our children's lives or those who have physical deformities should be taboo. These are some things that are off-limits in our family.

Practical jokes also have a limit. Used properly they become a fun life situation of their own by creating animation, but they should never have an intent to hurt or denigrate anyone. All family members have to learn to be careful that their jest doesn't turn into a mean "I'll get you back" attitude.

⤳ *Fragrant Tips from Gail* ⤳

"The happiest people are rarely the richest, or the most beautiful, or even the most talented," writes Jane Canfield. "Happy people do not depend on excitement and 'fun' supplied by externals. They enjoy the fundamental, often very simple, things of life. They waste no time thinking other pastures are greener. They do not yearn for yesterday or tomorrow. They savor the moment, glad to be alive, enjoying their work, their families, the good things around them. They are adaptable, they can bend with the wind, adjust to the changes in their times, enjoy the contests of life, and feel themselves in harmony with the world. Their eyes are turned outward, they are aware, compassionate. They have the capacity to love."[3]

God gives us only one life to live. I'm determined to create happy, fun, memorable events in our family to flavor circumstances.

Let's have some fun with the daily things we encounter as a parent and spouse. A creative eye will be able to size up any circumstance, inject a measure of fun in every situation, and intensify the sweetness of family fragrance. None of us can deny the words of Job—life is short and full of troubles—but that fact should not impede our efforts at merriment in the family. God gives us only one life to live on this earth. I'm determined to create happy, fun, and memorable events in our family to flavor circumstances when they become a bitter pill to swallow.

Care to join me?

Recipes For Merriment

LIVING ROOM CAMP OUT

Brian sets up the 6' x 6' pup tent in the family room Friday evenings throughout the year. In the winter, he and the two boys, six and four years old, have a campfire in the fireplace. They may even roast wieners or marshmallows. Sometimes they watch TV; other times they rent a video, then fall asleep with quiet conversation. What a great opportunity for Brian to ask and answer questions for his boys, and to touch their lives as a father!

ONE MORE KISS

Stephanie and her two little boys enjoy a game they call "One More Kiss." Tyler comes in for his goodnight kiss. When he crawls down off her lap and is walking away, she dramatically catches him and says, "No, don't go, gotta have one more kiss." She picks him up and smooches all over his face. He crawls down again and the scene is repeated five or six times before Mom is too tired. Then the second son wants the same treatment. The boys go away to bed giggling and happy. Stephanie settles down with good feelings for the evening.

WAITRESS MOM

Getting the children to the breakfast table used to be a trial for Sherry, until she came up with the fun idea of turning her breakfast room into a restaurant. She drapes a towel over her arm, sticks on a name tag, and, escorting the giggling kids to their seats, she asks, "And what would you like to order, sir?"

"Do you have any cereal?" comes the reply.

"Why certainly. Would you like milk on that, sir?"

"Please."

When the kids ask for things that are not allowed for breakfast, like ice cream or a Coke, she just replies, "Sorry, we are fresh out of that." The kids giggle and morning battles are kept at a minimum. In fact, this simple ritual of merriment impacts the rest of the day.

Lynn sets up the kitchen bar as a drive-through. The kids (one is the driver, and one is the passenger) order on one side of the bar then "drive" around to the other side and pick up their food!

Who hasn't gathered around the piano at Grandma's house and belted out a song? We imagine a bonfire and sing, "Kum Ba Yah." We are Elvis, the Beatles, Sinatra, The Tabernacle Choir all rolled into one.

HEALTHY EATING

Joe and Cindy are slowly becoming vegetarians, limiting the meat they consume to fowl and fish. Their three children also join in on the healthy vegetable diet. How did they accomplish the seemingly impossible? Early in the lives of their children, when it seemed impossible to get the kids to eat cauliflower and broccoli, Cindy decided to make it fun. She allowed the children to acquire a taste for different salad dressings. A small cup of their favorite dressing placed in front of them—even at snack time—did the trick. The smallest child thinks it is big stuff to dip his own broccoli stems into the dressing. The kids eventually preferred broccoli and cauliflower for snacks than most anything, if given a choice.

SINGING MAKES FOR MERRY HEARTS

The kindergarten teacher at our Christian school carries a guitar into her room filled with five year olds. She believes that singing is an important way for children to learn and have fun. Who hasn't gathered around the piano at Grandma's house and belted out a song? Our family does. We try to remember the title songs to old TV programs. We imagine a bonfire and sing, "Kum Ba Yah." We are Elvis, the Beatles, Sinatra, the Tabernacle Choir all rolled into one. Nursery rhymes and Sunday School songs are important because children learn principles by the words they memorize set to a tune. We compiled a list of songs for you to share with your children listed on page 165-166.

BREAKFAST PICNIC

Like all parents, we are looking to overcome the "B" word when it comes to family meals. When things seem a little boring, get up early, fix and pack up your family's favorite breakfast, then gently rouse the sleepers. Just don't head for the breakfast table. Head for the garage, get on your bikes (or walk) to the nearest neighborhood park, and picnic! It is refreshing to enjoy the cool air of a crisp morning, fun conversation, and a game or two.

ALL-NIGHT PICNIC

One family told us they would sometimes tell their children on Monday that something special was going to happen one night that week. Then on a given night, Mom and Dad gathered up a great picnic basket full of good food and junk food, gathered the rest of the family, and everyone went to one unsuspecting child's room at bedtime. They knocked on the door, and when invited in, all burst into the room with the basket of food, games, the unsuspecting child's favorite CD's, and everyone's sleeping bags. They had a late night picnic, told stories, went over picture albums, reminisced, and then all spent the night together in that child's room.

Plan a joke on somebody— J. Otis' secretary loves to tell of the time she and the youth pastor borrowed a life-size mannequin, dressed her in just a few fig leaves, and left her in the church office on April Fool's Day.

RAINY DAYS

Rainy day boxes are great items to have ready around your house. They give the kids something to look forward to when the weather turns dreary and Mom feels the house has become a gymnasium. Get a cardboard box for each child and fill it with special items that can only be used on an inclement day: preserved snacks (perhaps something that they rarely get on any ordinary day), and supplies suited for crafts (glue, paper, cellophane and double-sided tape, magazines for pictures, postcards, Christmas cards, stickers, old calendars, buttons, beads, lace, Popsicle sticks, pipe cleaners, Styrofoam, art supplies, leaves, shells, pebbles, pinecones, twigs, Silly Putty, string, even leftover wallpaper). Put the box in any out-of-the-way place marked with each child's name. Guaranteed . . . your children will pray for rain!

Designate a good weather day to get the kids together and let them make their own rainy day box. Or you may have them create such a box to take to an underprivileged child.

You can also prepare and bake something with your children during the gray day, and then enjoy it with tea when their projects are finished, using your best teacups.

NEW YEAR'S EVE PARTIES

Before our parents or other family members moved out to California, we celebrated New Year's, Christmas, Thanksgiving, and other holidays with several other ministerial families who were also without family. Make your own fun for your kids with what you've got. Some of our friends are more like aunts and uncles to our children than their own blood relatives.

Several families we know get together and eat, play games, eat, have competitions, eat, watch television and videos, and eat some more all night. The adults fix a huge breakfast for everyone to enjoy just when the sun is coming up. After breakfast, everyone goes home sleepy, happy, and stuffed.

Other familes have a Progressive Dinner beginning late New Year's Eve and ending in the early morning hours of the New Year. They sometimes have a theme and dress and prepare food accordingly. They have even done it backwards, starting with dessert and ending with appetizers. And, of course, then dress backwards!

❦

JANICE'S TEA PARTY

Our neighbor Janice, who had only one son, wanted to enjoy some "girl stuff." She invited four little neighborhood girls, all about the same age, over to a real tea party. The only stipulation was that they had to wear a hat and gloves along with their Sunday best. She kept the tradition annually until they began to move away. Our youngest, Leah, enjoyed it immensely.

❦

Year Round Ledbetter Traditions

THANKS FOR THE MEMORIES

Our children, Gail, and I love to indulge in telling stories of our past. It has a way of connecting our children to their personal history. They learn that their mom and I did date, and it wasn't in a buggy. They learn I'm not the only boy she ever dated, we had to do homework, too, and that their mom was a spunky cheerleader in college.

Our children are always interested, also, in knowing some of the headaches they caused us. They love hearing about how they may have embarrassed us at times with their antics, or how the hamster didn't die of natural causes, or that barking spiders really don't exist. We are always glad to oblige a story. Some of the stories take on a legendary quality and grow with the telling. Even today our married son and daughter will say, "Hey, Dad, tell the story about when . . ."

J. Otis

HAPPY BIRTHDAY OFF-KEY

Nobody can sing it worse than us. Somewhere in the merriment of past days, it became the thing to do. On any family member's birthday, they can expect to hear the harsh, dissonant, off-key, loud-as-a-gander honk serenade of the traditional happy birthday song. If it happens at a fast food restaurant, we sure draw lots of attention.

SUNDAY DINNER

Sunday dinner is a major event in our family. We are celebrating the Lord's Day, and it is the one day a week that we all know we are going to be with the people we deeply care about. It's a rhythmic meeting of the entire family and is rarely missed by anyone—it is too important. It includes the three of us, Matt and Joy, Becky and Justin, Grandpa and Grandma Hover, and usually Tom and Kristin (a couple we have extended our heritage to) and their two boys—thirteen in all. If for some reason one couple can't make it, we use the opportunity to extend our heritage to others.

The table is set for company Saturday night with all our finest. The meal is basically the same each week. Everyone complains if anything is changed. Arriving after Sunday morning worship, each person has a job, and we have backups in case anyone is absent or delayed. It doesn't take long to get everything on the table.

If someone celebrates a birthday that week, cards and gifts are piled on their plate. At prayer time, J. Otis purposely asks Grandpa Hover (being the patriarch) to pray while we all hold hands. It can get pretty noisy afterwards!

HEARTS ON LUNCH BAGS

I have always felt that making lunches for school and work was one of my least favorite things. Then I realized if that was going to be the worst thing that happened to me, my day was going to be pretty good! So I really tried to be creative with them and make them special. If my adolescent was having a difficult time with fair-weather friends, then seeing hearts or smoochy lips drawn all over her lunch bag would subtly remind her that someone did love her very much. I drew big eyes with long eyelashes on her bag sending her a butterfly kiss, even before the song became popular. She may have rolled her eyes in front of her friends at Mom's antics, but it still gave her pleasure. And it was nice for her to hear, "Your mom always makes the best lunches!"

Our Annual Traditions

JANUARY

NEW YEAR'S DAY

Several days throughout the year, our married kids come back home and spend the night in their old rooms. We even bunk out in the living room sometimes, and spend the night in front of the fireplace. New Year's Eve is never celebrated in the same way, but we always stay up late, eat special foods, sleep in late, eat a large breakfast with everyone helping out before we start on our day's activities.

SNOW FUN

Whether you have to go to the snow like we do here in California, or you live in it all winter, plan special days for fun in the snow with your family. Go skiing, cross-country skiing, skating, tobogganing and sledding, or just throw snowballs and make "angels." (And if you live in the Southwest, we have seen some very interesting "snowmen" made out of tumbleweeds painted white.)

While we've got you thinking, fill in *your* favorite family tradition for this month:

_____

_____

_____

_____

FEBRUARY
VALENTINE'S DAY

This may be the day when Dad pampers everyone. J. Otis used to buy each child a box of candy and a bigger one for Mom. Sometimes we ate out, but usually we ate, decorated, and planned a party at home—Valentine's Day is also Becky's birthday. You can plan a special breakfast, put special notes and surprises in lunches, pack red napkins, and plan something extra for dinner. The weather is still cold, so take advantage of candles and the fireplace. Emphasize love and romance. Make homemade, but beautiful, valentine cards together the week before the holiday.

Concerning school parties, make a card or food treat for every student in your child's class, not just for his friends. Valentine's Day can be very painful for children not considered part of the "in crowd."

PRESIDENT'S DAY

Whether you celebrate Lincoln's and Washington's birthdays separately or in one holiday (President's Day) as we do

in our school district, *plan* to make it memorable by making
a break in your normal routines: go out to lunch, shop at an
antique mall, go to the mountains, or skate on the lake.

Our favorite family tradition for February is:

_____

_____

_____

_____

MARCH
A DAY FOR FLYING KITES
Make or buy them, but take an afternoon or plan an annual
Saturday to fly kites in a neighborhood park, on the beach,
or from a mountaintop. Top it off with hot chocolate and
doughnuts or your favorite treat.

ST. PATRICK'S DAY
Dress all in green and serve corned beef and cabbage or
another Irish traditional food for dinner. Frost cupcakes with
white icing, and decorate with green sprinkles. Put up green
festoons. Practice your Irish accent, and sing "O Danny
Boy."

Our favorite family tradition for March is:

_____

_____

_____

_____

APRIL
APRIL FOOL'S DAY
Plan a joke on somebody or several people. Involve the family, or keep it a secret. My secretary loves to tell of the time she and the youth pastor borrowed a life-size mannequin and dressed her in just a few fig leaves. They looked awfully busy that April Fool's day as I walked through the outer office into mine. Seeing a half-dressed woman staring back at me when I flipped the light switch was quite a jolting experience. They not only saw my surprised reaction, they set up a video camera so everyone else could enjoy my astonishment. Caught on camera, there was no denying my shock.

J. Otis

EASTER
Enjoy Easter egg hunts and baskets full of candy, but emphasize the death of God's Son for us and celebrate His resurrection.

Sunrise Service. Our church congregation watches the sun come up together, gathers for a smorgasbord breakfast, and worships together.

Easter Services. Enjoy an Easter cantata at your own house of worship or earlier in the week at another. The family may celebrate by getting new clothes. After Sunday dinner, we plan something together with friends because there is usually not an evening service.

Easter Eggs. Our kids made beautifully dyed Easter eggs, and made white eggs into rabbits with cottontails, pink ears, and whiskers with their Grandma Hover each year. Our children didn't go on a "hunt," but they played with the eggs until they cracked or broke.

Our favorite family tradition for April is:

_____

_____

_____

_____

MAY
MOTHER'S DAY
Plan a Mother/Daughter banquet for your church, enjoy church services together with Mom, and take her out for dinner or tea at a special place.

MEMORIAL DAY
This holiday signals the end of school and the coming of summer. We usually spent the day with another family from Southern California—they visited us, or our family went there. We took sleeping bags and all camped out together in their huge upstairs. They have also rented a beach house and we spent the day at the ocean. When they came here, we've gone to nearby Yosemite National Park, to mountain villages, or swimming at a friend's pool.

Our favorite family tradition for May is:

_____

_____

_____

_____

JUNE
GRADUATIONS
Support family and friends by remembering their graduations.

Send cards or gifts, have parties, and go to their graduation if possible. Many churches recognize graduates in services and have them wear their gowns. If so, suggest your youth director tell about any honors or scholarships they have received; see if the graduates can give testimonies and share future plans.

FATHER'S DAY

Somehow, Mother's Day is more sentimental, and Father's Day is a time of fun. Plan a day just for Dad and Grandpa. After church, fix a favorite dish, or go to a favorite restaurant. Celebrate by going miniature golfing, bowling, to the batting cages, or to the park.

Our favorite family tradition for June is:

_____

_____

_____

_____

JULY, AUGUST
THE FOURTH OF JULY

A big celebration for us, it's also Matthew's birthday. We always hang the flag out and are thankful for our Christian heritage. At nightfall, we join others at our youth director's house next to the local high school where we eat homemade ice cream and watch the fireworks go off at the stadium.

FUN IN THE SUN

Be intentional about planning summer activities with your family. We go camping, to the beach, miniature golfing, antiquing at our favorite country villages, or take short trips on the Amtrak train. We plant a garden, go on picnics, visit friends, work on a project together, paint a room, do crafts, plan our layout for our Christmas village, go to Little League games, involve ourselves in coed sports, support our community summer theater, and go to our local farmer's market. Whatever you do, enjoy life when you don't have the pressures of school.

Our favorite family traditions for summer are:

_____

_____

_____

_____

SEPTEMBER
LABOR DAY
The last holiday of the summer, we make it memorable by usually playing our traditional Family Baseball. Last time, we bought a game ball and had everyone sign it with their nicknames. We'll leave it on display all year, and then get another one for next year. Consider starting an annual activity that your family loves.

BACK TO SCHOOL
Make buying new clothes fun instead of a battlefield. Lunch at a local restaurant while shopping. Plan some activities to help your children become better prepared for school. Invite their new friends over to your home. Send pizza to school for your child's whole class (let him be the hero of the day— be sure to check with his teacher first).

EVENING WALKS

When the air begins to get crisp, we go for night walks together. It gives opportunites for talking without distractions.

Our favorite family tradition for September is:

_____

_____

_____

_____

OCTOBER

GATHERING FALL LEAVES

We made an annual trip into the mountains when the leaves began to change colors after the first frost. The trip yielded beautiful colored leaves, pinecones, and other items with which to decorate our mantle and home. Depending on which direction we headed, we ended up having hot chocolate at our favorite chalet or enjoyed delights at the apple farm with warm cider and hot apple pie. We brought home bushels of apples.

At home, we added pumpkins, Indian corn, and gourds to our treasures. We taped leaves to the bricks on our fireplace. The best part of our trip, though, was our time together in the car. We had great discussions, made plans for the coming holiday season, and enjoyed being together. No one wanted the day to end.

OCTOBERFESTS

We go to local celebrations and craft fairs, and enjoy the regional food. Our men are happier about going on these shopping outings because they get ideas for Christmas.

HALLOWEEN

Make Halloween fun once again for your children. We have parties, instead of trick-or-treating in places where we're not familiar. Check with neighborhood churches to see if they are planning alternative parties. (See *Holiday Family Nights,* Jim Weidmann/Kurt Bruner, Chariot Victor.)

Our favorite family tradition for October is:

_____

_____

_____

_____

NOVEMBER

THANKSGIVING

Research the truth of the first Thanksgiving in the fall of 1623, and the significance of the five kernels of corn. (See William Bradford's *Of Plymouth Plantation* at your local library.) Don't depend on the revisionists to give you the truth of our Christian American holiday.

Give thanks. Whether you travel to Grandma's, eat at home, or celebrate with friends, make this a special day for your family, using your very best of everything. Have everyone join in on the preparations. Have the children creatively decorate your table and fold the napkins into new shapes. And don't forget the less fortunate; like many others, our church has a food drive for needy families.

FRIDAY AFTER THANKSGIVING

At our house, this is one of the most significant days of the year. We celebrate Christmas the whole month of December, and need to get an early start. We start out the day with a big breakfast at our home, and then with several families head for the Christmas tree farms. We end up buying six or seven trees among the several families, and sometimes go to three or four farms to get just the right ones. At home, we hose ours down, spray it with bug spray to get rid of pests, and let it dry. On Saturday morning, we bring it in and put on the white lights. It will take most of the day to decorate because the tree is always over ten feet tall.

We have begun a new tradition in the last few years, popping in the family videos we made of Christmases past when the kids were very small. We watch them all in sequence, ending with last year's. We'll stop and watch different parts and laugh until we can't breathe!

Our favorite family tradition for November is:

_____

_____

_____

_____

_____

DECEMBER
ADVENT CALENDAR
Begin an advent calendar on the first of December. Buy or make one for each child. It will help them count down to Christmas Day, enhancing their sense of anticipation.

DECORATING
The first week, decorate every room in the house. The older children always had Christmas lights surrounding their windows in their bedrooms. We left the lights on until they fell asleep, and turned them on again when we woke the children

in the morning. The last several years, we have stapled a huge Christmas tree of lights and tinsel on Leah's bedroom wall.

OUT-OF-TOWN PACKAGES
If you exchange gifts with relatives out-of-town, spread out the fun. If a big package came, we would eat dinner and open the gifts that night.

CHRISTMAS CAROLING
Plan a night to go caroling with friends at hospitals, senior citizen homes, to shut-ins, or on a walk in your neighborhood. Take bags of decorated Christmas cookies for each stop.

HOLIDAY PERFORMANCES
Go to community and church performances of *The Messiah*. Some communities have sing-alongs. Take the whole family to see *The Nutcracker* or *A Christmas Carol.*

COOKIE DECORATING
Bake lots of cut-out cookies, and have family and friends over to decorate them. Use white frosting and food coloring. Have lots of nuts, candies, and toppings to add.

SEASONAL TV SPECIALS
Look up your favorites in the television guide, invite family and friends over to enjoy them together.

CHRISTMAS MORNING
We always allowed our children to break into their bulging stockings hanging from the mantle as soon as they woke up Christmas morning. That kept them occupied until we ate a

big breakfast, then began opening our gifts from one another. It is our custom to take turns opening gifts, one at a time—it usually takes us about an hour and a half. That way it lasts longer, and everyone gets to see everything.

CHRISTMAS NIGHT
Intentionally plan something for Christmas night. Otherwise, after all the anticipation, the gifts, the huge meal, and the fun, it can be a let down. Plan something simple but easy to do—have a Scrabble (or pick any table game) tournament, view a movie, get together with friends.

Our favorite family tradition for December is:

_____

_____

_____

_____

_____

→ Chapter 6 ←

Affirmation: The Blended Fragrance

Affection

Respect

Order

Merriment

Affirmation

The six-foot-two, normally reserved Lyn Golden is jumping up and down, flinging his long arms in the air, and cheering at the very top of his lungs. He is cheering for his five-year-old son, Mikel, who is competing in his first BMX bicycle race. Everything seems all right on the sidelines, but something is terribly wrong on the track. Mikel is in last place. In fact, he's the only rider left in the race. The others have put away their bikes and are already celebrating with their families. Some are opening picnic baskets and beginning to eat. Mikel is still on the track.

Lyn bought the BMX equipment, knowing his son had his heart set on this race. Now it is about to be a disaster. Lyn can hear Mikel's staccato sobbing as the bumpy track jars his little body. The tears cut a river bed down his cheeks. Reaching to wipe them away, Mikel's face streaks with dried mud. Still half-a-lap to go!

Lyn, the only person left in the gallery, is going nuts—as if Mikel is in first place. When Mikel finally crosses the finish line, Lyn grabs him in his arms and continues the celebration.

"I'm so proud of you, Son," Lyn shouts. Mikel starts smiling through his tears.

There are two first-place winners today. One is awarded a trophy, the other affirmed with relationship. Mikel's first place position is declared loud and clear from the heart of his dad. It was a position that Mikel has always had, today declared true.

J. Otis

Affirmation
is an established, clearly held position declared as true.[1]

We've all been there, haven't we? We have felt the pain of our children when they have lost, and we want them to know more than anything that losing really doesn't matter. There will be another day to win a race, but they are winners in our hearts just because they belong to us. How are we affirmed as children of our Heavenly Father? Are we affirmed by what He gives to us?

Are we affirmed by whether the day is a good day? Then what about a bad day? Do we feel affirmed only if everything is going our way? Well, maybe *we* experience affirmation these ways, but those are not the real measures. The true measure of affirmation is based on our Father's attributes. He is love. He is faithful. He is just and merciful. He watches over us constantly. He

> *The true measure of affirmation is based on our Father's attributes. He is love. He is faithful. He is just and merciful. His character is our affirmation. That is the model.*

cares for us deeply and has promised never to leave or forsake us. His *character* is our affirmation. That is the model.

Of course, along with affirmation come its by-products: gifts, having a good day, or knowing that a bad day isn't the end of all days, believing everything is going our way even when it may not be, having our question marks turned into exclamation points, and knowing that our true position with God makes everything okay, even if things do not turn out according to our expectations.

Aroma is an upward spiral _____

PRINCIPLE: Affirmation results from affection, respect, order, and merriment. It is the apex of *AROMA.*

INTENTIONAL IMPACT: To allow our children to know who they are and whose they are.

How can a family illustrate affection, respect, order, and merriment within a single setting? Wayne and Janet Byrd found a solution at the dinner table. Janet purchased a china plate with the words "You are loved" and "You are special" painted along the outer rim. On each of the six family members' birthdays, the plate is set at the head of the table where the guest of honor is seated and esteemed for the night. A favorite meal is prepared, and the other family members tell something they appreciate about the honoree. Even Mom and Dad look forward to their special day.

"To hear the family display a grateful spirit is riveting," Janet says.

"There are even times when there are tears of joy. At our oldest son's birthday, our youngest recounted how he was being teased about a private matter at school. Wayne and I were unaware of it until that night at the table. We found out our oldest was riding his bike to the youngest's school every day after classes to take him home, stopping for a soda and some important talks. As parents, we were moved to hear how affirming that incident became to their lives.
                                                                        J. Otis

When all previous ingredients of *AROMA* are intact, affirmation falls naturally into its proper place. Like the elusive butterfly, when you cease chasing, it lights on your shoulder. Affirmation need not be tirelessly pursued; it is the natural, sweet aroma that emerges when the other four parts of family fragrance are collectively blended.

Children have an innate desire to belong, an insatiable need to connect. They will search for a niche with a relentless pursuit until they find the place where they fit. If they don't find it in the family, but find it in a gang, that's fine with them. They are not created hermits. They want to know where connection will take place. Their search will not be assuaged until that question is answered. When affirmation comes naturally, if children are allowed the freedom to know and be comfortable with who they are and with the people to whom they belong, an identity crisis can be avoided.

Affirmation spotlights the positive _____

PRINCIPLE: Affirmation or condemnation happens in every family.

INTENTIONAL IMPACT: To make affirmation happen in a positive setting in our home as opposed to the negative.

I have heard it called "The door of affirmation," and I have heard it called "The gallery of affirmation." Whatever you call your refrigerator door, it is certainly a great place to affirm children. Little Suzy's first drawing held with magnets and clever sayings, gives us encouragement. Receipts, bank deposits, pictures of folks barely remembered, magazine articles, obituaries, and "stick um" notes all are fastened to the door. The neighborhood kids are even given a showing. Whatever you use yours to display, always make room for those important papers brought home by your fledgling artist and authors. Matthew walked past the refrigerator the first time Gail stuck his effort at finger painting on "the door," wearing a permanent grin. His little chest stuck out farther than it ever had before. Not many places in your house bring more affirmation.

J. Otis

In every home, a child will either be affirmed that he does belong or does not belong. Some parents affirm belonging with a negative reinforcement, however. While that may have its place, too much may be misconstrued as unwarranted criticism from parents. There is a place for the "thou shalt nots" in every family, concise and clear, just like the Ten Commandments. But Gail and I found while spirits sagged under the law of the negative, our children flourished under the grace of positive reinforcement. We wrote a "Bill of Rights" for our children. It became positive reinforcement, our affirmation of them.

Every child has a right:

1. TO EMOTIONAL STABILITY. Every day of childhood should bring fondness, not fear. Family times and memories should warm the child's heart, not tighten his stomach. Expressed affection brings an environment of safety

and love where emotional health is fostered. The key to this is unconditional love, and nurturing the family fragrance.

2. TO LIVE IN AN AFFIRMING ENVIRONMENT. Your child should be surrounded by a world full of possibilities, not a hostile environment. Help by affirming safety. Do your part to promote a safe neighborhood, physically and emotionally, by supporting neighborhood watches. Walk down the sidewalk and meet your neighbors. Building neighborhood relationships helps create an affirmimg environment, and that will help your home flourish.

. . . . .

Every child has the right to:

Emotional stability
Live in an affirming environment
Pursue their potential
Make mistakes
Know truth
Free time on their own
Receive nurture and admonition
Grow in responsibility
Grow in knowledge
Be hugged

. . . . .

3. TO PURSUE THEIR POTENTIAL. Kids deserve the right not to be maneuvered or exploited by parents who have an agenda (such as sports or the arts) that is not in the child's best interest. Finding and developing personal interests and talents are the building blocks for a stable life. Every

child has natural talents. The only way for parents to know what they are is to give children freedom to explore and be curious. From a variety of talents, certain aptitudes will eventually emerge.

4. TO MAKE MISTAKES. There is no success without failure. There is no teaching without tests. If children have no problems, they will never know how to solve them. Give your children plenty of room for mistakes. Of course, some mistakes, like substance abuse or choosing wrong friends, should be avoided, but garden-variety mistakes can be dynamic teaching grounds between parent and child. The parent's job is holding the child accountable and being there when needed.

5. TO KNOW TRUTH. Truth is what you find when your attitudes, predispositions, and beliefs are measured by an objective standard. We believe that standard is the Holy Bible. Every child deserves the right to be able to access that reservoir of wisdom.

6. TO THEIR OWN FREE TIME. Happy kids are not coerced by the busy schedules of their parents. Your children need time to think, play, be creative, pursue hobbies and wishes, imagine, and pretend to be anything and anybody they want to be. This does not preclude chores, but does balance responsibility and play.

7. TO RECEIVE NURTURE AND ADMONITION. Discipline is learned through nurture and admonition. Nurture appeals to a child's conscience through emotion and intellect. Admonition appeals to a child's conscience through physical consequences such as restriction, loss of free-

doms, or proper spankings. Children learn to reason through life's circumstances. Emphasis should be on nurturing. Success in this area will result in rare physical punishment.

8. TO GROW IN RESPONSIBILITY. Picking up toys, cleaning their rooms, and making their beds are all areas where children can begin learning to be responsible. It is not unrealistic to expect a school-age child to help around the house for thirty minutes a day. Not only does it teach responsibility, it also promotes a sense of belonging by making them feel essential in the daily scheme of things.

9. TO GROW IN KNOWLEDGE. The learning of facts and figures is vital to strengthening basic skills. Find a good school. Get to know the teacher. Get involved in your children's classes. Don't take for granted that because you drop them off every morning, learning becomes automatic. Look at their homework. Ask for progress reports. Hold child and teacher accountable for a good education.

10. TO BE HUGGED. You've heard the old adage, "An apple a day keeps the doctor away." We say, "A hug a day, keeps family indifference at bay." When the family dog runs to you wagging his tail, licks your hand, and excitedly jumps because he is glad to see you, it's not hard to respond in a joyous manner. Of course, a child is not a family pet, but when he is hugged, squeezed, loved, and affirmed, it is hard for him to be indifferent. The natural reaction is to respond in kind.

The Fragrance of Affirmation—Guidelines

1. Learn and use phrases that foster family connection.

. . . . .

A child who hears love in his parent's words feels tethered to family, which is a secure position from where they can discover the rest of the world.

. . . . .

Encouragement that is not solicited serves the family well. It is the unexpected, out-of-the-blue phrases that make children tingle with the delight of affirmation:

"You know, I really do love you."

"You are my favorite (you fill it in)."

"I'm glad that I'm your Daddy/Mama."

"What did I do to deserve such a great son/daughter?"

"You are a delight to your mom and me."

Simple phrases like these say, "you belong in this family." It helps children draw on our wellspring of love for them. A child who hears love in his parents' words feels tethered to family, which is a secure position from where they can discover the rest of their world.

2. Use the power of touch.

The hand is a powerful tool. It can represent abuse or it can represent affection. Kurt Bruner and I wrote about the power of the hand in our book *Your Heritage:* "Touch is a tangible reminder of love. It feels good and it means much when we receive it, whether a hand on the shoulder, a rub on the back, or a warm kiss."[2] Nothing—absolutely nothing—can fill the emptiness in a child's life from physically distant parents. God gave us the extremities called hands and arms partly to demonstrate esteem and affirmation. So envelop children in your arms. Set them on your lap. Tousle their hair with tenderness. Rub their shoulders and backs as if without thinking. Hold their hands. Stroke their faces with your fingertips. Lie beside them on the floor as they watch cartoons and laugh with them. Be creative with your power called touch.

3. Major on positive reinforcement

Each of us will collect negative reinforcement in our walk through every day in the big bad world. Home should be the place to balance experience with positive reinforcement. Use uplifting phrases when you catch your child doing something right, or want to help when he has made a mistake:

"I trust you."
"You are first in my book."
"You will give it your best, I'm sure."
"Follow your dreams."
"I will support you in your efforts."
"You may be down now, but I know you won't stay there."

Some parents jam verbal reinforcements with sarcasm. Sarcasm as humor has its place, we suppose, but should be used sparingly and carefully. Overuse can cause damage when sarcasm becomes a habit. It can be hard for a child to rise above its negative tone. Frequently, sarcasm is the saccharin of communication in family—a substitute for the real thing. It may be palatable and seem jovial at first, but frequently leaves a bitter aftertaste. It can make a child feel insecure, then makes it easy for him to retort with sarcasm because it contains a rebellious edge. Positive, uplifting phrases become a conversational model for children to follow that makes them feel good.

4. Communicate clearly.

When affirming, over-communicate. Performing solo on the platform for the first time was a frightening experience. I was sure that I wore a smiling, pleasant countenance, but when I watched a video of the performance, I saw what everyone else did. I had a smile on the inside, but an apathetic, or should I say, pathetic look outside. I quickly learned to over-communicate positive feelings through my facial expressions. Then enthusiasm came across to the audience. In a similiar manner, we may feel we are communicating, but our message never reaches others. Speak clearly, with more emotion than seems needed, to make sure those you love know your deep feelings for them. Under-communication or non-communication is later regrettable, while those who use over-communication rarely suffer emotional periods of regret.

5. Eliminate all hurtful name calling.

Our family loves to engage in playful name calling. Used properly, it is pretty affirming. Many of us have affectionate nicknames, don't we? Some of them even stay with us all of our lives, and that's okay. But hurtful name calling should have no place in our family vocabularies. Names that point out physical flaws like "Fatso" or "Scarface," or emotional flaws like "Mamma's Boy" or "Stupid" are inexcusable even if done in jest. The best rule of thumb is to simply eliminate potentionally hurtful names completely.

Fragrant Tips from Gail

Spouses who have been in love for a long time don't fret over needing reassurance of each other's love, but when offered freely and unexpectedly, affirmation is so enriching. Children who have been loved lavishly since birth still enjoy—and at times need—the reassuring smooch at send-off to pre-school, the bear hug after a hard day at elementary school, and the wink in public across a crowded room before a recital in high school. The old adage says, "When people *Act, Walk,* and *Look* like leaders, people follow." We believe that when we *Act, Walk,* and *Look* at our children like we love them, they will be affirmed and flourish.

Speak with more emotion than seems needed to make sure those you love know your deep feelings for them.

God lavishes affection, respects us, orders our world, and delights us with unspeakable joy constantly. He didn't just say, "Of course I love you" *once,* and that was the end of it. He constantly affirms us over and over by such things as answering our prayers, staying closer than a brother, fulfilling promises and prophecies, opening our hearts and minds to new and deeper concepts as we study His Word, and giving us inward peace in an unpeaceful world. Parents love their children in the same way: we affirm them by *constantly* reminding them of our love, by giving them respect, by surrounding their lives with an orderly rhythm, and by making family a fun place in which to come home. If I had to list individual tips on how to affirm our children, I would have to list again all the ideas shared in the last four chapters: ditto, ditto, ditto, ditto. Keep doing them over and over.

Affirming means to continue to do those things necessary for a child's spiritual, emotional, and social growth. It doesn't stop when they become legally responsible for themselves at age eighteen. My parents still affirm me today, and I will continue to be a parent who my children will be able to come to as long as I live. So instead of naming again those things that need to be affirmed, we want to ask *what* things need to be affirmed in your loved ones' lives?

Our children need to know that there is nothing they can do to make God love them less, and there is nothing they can do to make God love them more.

Whose they are—God's and ours

Our children need to know that there is nothing they can do to make God love them less, and there is nothing they can do to make God love them more. That knowledge alone can take a big load off a child. But they must also know that their parents feel the same way about them. That doesn't imply children should quit striving for excellence, nor does it give them license to do whatever they please. In this very negative world that has a bent toward knocking down the child or teen who tries to excel, parents need to be involved and ready to reassure a troubled child of God's unconditional love and their own abiding love for them.

Can there be a greater illustration of this truth than the prodigal son of Luke 15? He was absent physically from the father, but not positionally. He entertained wrong friends, slept with harlots, and rooted with the hogs. When he decided to go home, he wasn't sure of his position—but his father was. The conversation in the middle of the road when he was almost home did not contain the subject of the diseases he may now have, or the duration of his long absence, or of debt. Make no mistake about it, there was loss on the son's part, but that isn't the issue. The point is that on the father's part, there was only affirmation of the son's position in the family. He still belonged.

Our children responded to our early efforts at affirmation when they saw either their lastest or earliest picture thoughtfully placed in a strategic place in the home, or when they saw their name written on something and placed in a prominent position. Remember how your children strutted proudly around when you attached their first attempt at art or writing on the refrigerator door or bathroom mirror? If yours are like ours were, they will walk past it a hundred times within the first half hour of the display. This says volumes to them about who they are and where they belong. It is so simple, yet so powerful.

A family told me about the perpetual tree that sits in their family room and is decorated for all kinds of holiday festivities. During the month of each of the family members' birthdays (including Mom's and Dad's), the tree is decorated in honor of the person whose birthday they are celebrating. The simplest accomplishments are noted on handmade ornaments and hung on the tree. Medals they have won, and awards received are hung or displayed on the limbs. Children are encouraged to think of a character quality they like about their sibling, and symbolize it by creating an ornament to bring to the tree. For example, unselfishness could be symbolized by creating a heart with family members drawn inside of it, indicating the person has room in her heart for all of them.

Thoughtfulness *could be symbolized as a wrapped gift box and indicated by writing the word giving on its ribbon. If baseball or soccer is their passion, then the tree could easily reflect their*

love for that sport. Scores of ideas will pop into the minds of partic-
ipants as they prepare to affirm a family member for the month
through the family tree. The beautiful thing about this tree is that
it is a positive influence on all family members as they focus on the
good traits of each other.

J. Otis

Who they are
Sexually

Today's adolescent needs accurate answers to the age-old
questions: Who am I? Why am I here? Where am I going?
This is especially true concerning their sexuality. We live in a
confused world where it's "cool" to be homo- or bi-sexual,
where purity is ridiculed, abstinence is viewed as unwork-
able, and foundational biblical standards are judged as intol-
erant or even homophobic.

As we see it, parents have a few choices here. We can: (1)
Curse the darkness. (2) Not rock the boat (allowing our children to attend the sex-education classes and trying to undo
the damage after the fact). (3) Be open-minded and hope our
children make the right choices. (4) Be pro-active in helping
our child know who he or she is, sexually. In this world
where anything and everything is openly discussed in mixed
company in the classroom, on television, or in the halls of
Congress, parents have got to get involved. For our children's sake, we must get over our own embarrassment, protect them and their natural reticence whenever we can, and
give them the freedom to openly discuss their concerns with
us whenever they have a question. Their sexual health is too
important to leave it to chance. In fact, I wanted to be the
one to talk to each of them, and would not have been happy
if someone else had first.

I talked with each of our three children easily and openly when they began to ask questions about their bodies and how babies got here. I let them ask questions—some were pretty humorous—and eliminated wrong information they had gotten from school children. I had a few rules I followed: I didn't give out personal information about their father or me, but rather used general information. I didn't laugh or giggle or act embarrassed. I used both the technical terms for body parts (so that they would be familiar with accurate information), and our own "family names." I emphasized throughout the whole conversation that sex was God's idea first and that it was clean and beautiful.

Sometimes J. Otis and I had some great talks with our two oldest children together, because they were so close in age and had a lot of the same questions and concerns. Since sex was not a taboo subject in our home, it lost a lot of its negative intrigue.

With our son, I explained all the basics, and then his father did a follow up. Sometimes, he would come into our room and talk to both of us once he was comfortable no question was going to be ridiculed or rebuffed with "Don't talk about that—that's nasty."

Before our girls started menstruation, they got a demonstration about feminine products (and how to dispose of them neatly) so that they wouldn't have any surprises later. And just like other parts of our lives, this very personal part also hinges on attitude. Because the television and magazines scream, "Leave me alone; I have PMS!" doesn't mean that we have to behave that way. I teach my girls at the high school to have some reticence, some modesty, and even some mystique about their personal life. Just because something is normal and natural doesn't mean we have to inform the entire student body. "Girl talk" should be left there—

among the girls. I've heard a few girls announce what time of the month it is for them (usually as an excuse for bad behavior) and have seen the guys speechless, retort with another vulgarity, or be totally disgusted—and the other girls embarrassed. Because the world lets it all hang out, doesn't mean we shouldn't teach our girls to be ladies.

Our youngest was born many years after the other two. All four of us enjoyed watching her pass through each stage of growing up. When she began asking questions about reproduction, she and I made a date for a day later that week to talk about it. We both giggled and hugged all week, looking forward to the day. When it arrived, we first went to a beautiful park, held hands, and gathered fall leaves (we still have them). We talked about a lot of girl things in general. Then we went to a local restaurant, talked about specific things and drew lots of pictures until she finally ran out of questions. When we arrived home, Dad and our other children hugged her and spoke kindly—they didn't tease her about something so special. It was as if they brought her into an exclusive club of "the knowing."

Spiritually

Another thing that must be affirmed in a child's life is where he is going to spend eternity. Many children make a decision for Christ at a young age, and then begin to have doubts when they are teens. To us the solution is simple. Go through the plan of salvation again as if it were the first time. Don't allow Satan to get a foothold through confusion in young spiritual lives. If children were truly born again when they were young, going through God's plan again won't hurt anything. Both of our older kids became Christians as children, and both wanted "to just be sure" at youth camp as teens. We are dealing with eternity here; it is too important to be nonchalant about. A plan on how to lead your child to Christ is included at the end of this book.

Socially

When Jesus laid aside His royalty, He never doubted Whose He was. He first grew in favor with God and then with man. And as parents, it is not enough just to have our children become believers: We want them to also be committed Christians. It isn't possible to separate one's spiritual walk from one's social life. What a person believes is going to determine how a person lives. We don't want our children to follow the path of materialistic Christianity or to seek a God whose only job is to make them feel good. We do want them to know personally the God of the Bible Who is worthy of our devotion and love, Who is our All in All, and Whom we can trust to watch out for our good even when we don't understand.

We can create an environment where the Word of God has a chance to change our children. How can we say we believe in the reality of a life to come, but live only for this life that is going to pass away?

In a nation of easy-believism and noncommitment, Christians may experience ridicule, but few have faced persecution or death. Unlike believers in other countries, when we are baptized publically, few of us have been disinherited by our families. With our high standard of living and abundant time for recreation, many of us have come to expect our spiritual life to be easy also. It's easy to fall into the trap of expecting God to be a personal genie who waits to promptly grant our wishes. We have found that many of the people who quit the church don't do it because it was too hard, but rather because they feel God disappointed them.

There are no guarantees. People do have choices. After all, the perfect parent—God—had two rebellious children— Adam and Eve. But what might we do to improve the chances of our children in this world?

First, we must be committed ourselves. Nobody respects a hypocrite who lives out "Do as I say, not as I do." When we face a choice, do we take the easy road or the right road? Our children are watching, and they are not fooled even if they don't call us on it. If the Christian walk were easy, the way would be crowded. But it isn't crowded, and it isn't easy. Are we living for this life or for the life to come? Do we choose recreation over righteousness? Family over faith? Ease over edification?

Second, we can create an environment where the Word of God has a chance to change our children. Godliness needs to be acted out in the home through daily decision making, traditions, Family Nights, corporate worship, and Bible study. It is difficult for a child to rise above the negative example of parents who are casual Christians. How can we say we believe in the God of the Bible, but know next to nothing of that Bible? How can we say we believe in the reality of a life to come, but live only for this life that is going to pass away? These questions are frequently left unanswered, and they need to be answered for our children. As Americans experiencing The Good Life, we often want the results of Christianity—freedom, liberty, the Golden Rule, fair play—

but not the discipline of Christianity—commitment, vigilance, responsibility. We can't have it both ways; not in our national life, and not in our personal lives.

If we want our children to be growing Christians who are listening to God, and in turn impacting their world, we can't leave it to chance or to how we may be feeling at the time. We have to be committed first, and then commit to giving them every opportunity to allow God to touch their lives.

. . . . .

Intentional Touchpoints of Affirmation:
Mealtimes
Rituals and traditions
Bedtimes
Worship and Family Nights

. . . . .

Continuous affirmation
Here are some intentional touchpoints where you can constantly be affirming your children:

1. **Mealtimes** are a time of communication, reassurance, and comfort as well as nourishment.

2. **Rituals** of Sunday dinner and holiday celebrations teach sociability, good manners, the art of conversation, confidence, and predictability.

3. **Bedtimes** are the sweetness of relaxation after hard work.

4. **Order** means the lack of clutter physically, emotionally, and mentally. This requires vigilance (determination), good humor, and consistency. Order results in a good-natured, rhythmic flow within the family.

5. **Virtue** (J. Otis and I call it "virtuous reality") is expressed where moral enthusiasm, a decision to live according to God's guidelines, is tied to our sexual identity.

We want our children to know and practice virtue in every circumstance, so we affirm who they are in Christ.

6. Traditions and Family Nights serve to spawn companionship, and prepare us spiritually for the life to come in eternity.

7. Worship—God's Word says, ". . . not forsaking the assembling of ourselves together, as is the manner of some, but exhorting one another, and so much the more as you see the Day approaching" (Hebrews 10:25 NKJV). I don't want to be grouped with the "some" who are nonchalant about meeting in God's house. One of the greatest ways our children have been affirmed is by regular interaction with other committed Christians. Why substitute God's plan?

8. Touch—From the most reserved to the most vivacious, every individual needs meaningful, enthusiastic, deliberate, and frequent physical affirmation from those who love them most. It might be embraces, pats on the back, strokes on the face, high-fives, or teasing punches—just hug your family members as much as possible!

Epilogue
By Gail

The year is 1861 and the Civil War has already started. In November, at the beginning of the carnage, a boy is born in one of the border states—Kentucky. As best we've been able to find out, his mother is not married to his father, and it doesn't appear she even wants her son. During the war, and for years afterwards, he is passed among people who might have been relatives. As soon as he is able, he "hires out"—works for food and a place to sleep. He grows to be over six feet tall. He is not educated—he never learns to read or write. Any time he has to sign a legal paper, he marks it with an X. Years later, some nameless person tells him about the Lord Jesus Christ, and he becomes one of the Lord's followers.

When he is nineteen, another child is born. She, too, is reared in Kentucky, and they have something else in common— she thinks, because no one will discuss it, she is a bastard child, illegitimate, without family history. In fact, she will die believing it. But later research shows her grandchildren that her mother was young and immature, and that her parents did the unthinkable then—got a divorce. She is raised by her father's people. These Christians love her, educate her, and teach her to love God.

In 1900, when she is twenty years old, the young woman

meets and marries that tall man who is now almost twice her age. They love each other, determine to lay aside the sorrow of their pasts, and make a good life together. They have ten children, the last one born when the father is sixty-one years old. That baby is my mother.

That same year, a boy is born not far away in Missouri. He, also, is born into a Christian family of farmers with ten children. Child number nine is my dad. Life isn't easy—six years after he is born, the Great Depression begins. In December, 1941, when he is eighteen, the Japanese bomb Pearl Harbor. He and his brothers hear the news after church on the way to a sister's house for Sunday dinner. He goes home to the farm to find his mother crying—she has six sons. Three of them will eventually join the war effort, but meanwhile he moves to Detroit and connects with childhood friends who have found work in the wartime factories. He quickly gets involved in an active church.

My mother's family is living in Detroit since migrating during the Depression. She, along with her aging parents and married siblings, attend that same church. Here, Dad meets Mom, and soon they fall in love. They marry with my dad wearing his US Navy uniform. Eventually they have four daughters. I am daughter number two.

I share this to illustrate a deeply important point of life: we are all in the process of giving and receiving a heritage—that spiritual, emotional, and social legacy that is passed from parent to child for good or bad. I received a legacy from people who understood the importance of what they were passing. They realized they had a responsibility to offspring they would never know. Their attitudes, predispositions, and behaviorial patterns would stretch through future generations. They planted seeds that would grow into trees under whose shade they would never sit. They modeled what it means to let go of hurtful things and stumbling blocks, and look to future generations.

I was raised in a wonderful family in a busy, exuberant time for Americans. (We won the war!) My parents could have been the Cleavers, the Waltons, or Ozzie and Harriet. I was a very happy child surrounded by a huge extended family whose life centered around our church. For years my grandma got the award for having the most family present on Mother's Day. My parents were junior high Sunday School superintendents for twenty years. In 1955, when I was seven years old, *LIFE* magazine did an article about "the largest church in America" with an attendance of 6,300 and took a picture of the congregation for the centerfold. (It gives a whole new meaning to the word "centerfold" doesn't it!)

My dad was strict, but he loved children. I never heard him curse, and I was impressed with his God because my dad modeled and reinforced the unseen realities of the spiritual life. His God answered our family's prayers.

My dad was a hard worker and did a lot of overtime to support his wife and four daughters—ten hours a day, and five to eight hours on Saturday. He didn't work Sundays usually, but every now and then his tool and die shop would have to open extra hours when the automobile assembly lines changed models. Time was at a premium. *Everybody* had to work or shut down and not make schedule. Although Dad didn't want to, he would work Sundays for the sake of his employers. One of those times, Dad did something important to me as an impressionable adolescent, and he didn't even know it. He said, "I make double, sometimes triple time when I have to work on Sunday. We could sure use the money, but it's the Lord's Day. So along with my tithe, I give all of Sunday's wages to the Lord, too. It's His day." My dad was not living for this world's goods then, and today at seventy-five, he still does not. His eyes are on eternity, and his godly life is still pointing others to Jesus.

My dad and mom also knew how to have fun, and always

took vacations and holidays with their children. They created an enduring sense of security and emotional stability. They nurtured it in an environment of safety and love that comes with a healthy legacy. Life was happy, but it wasn't perfect. I suffered neighborhood rivalries, sibling squabbles, injustices at school by teachers and peers, and later, teenage heartaches. A younger sister had scoliosis during early adolescence and was in a body cast for a year and a half. My precious, invalid grandmother (who had married that thirty-nine-year-old bachelor) lived with us, and later had no memory. We had to introduce ourselves to her each day until she died the day before my seventeenth birthday.

But life is never perfect for any family. Each family and each individual have a choice—to allow life's hurts to make them bitter or make them better. My parents, and grandparents who had gone through societal shunning through no fault of their own, endured poverty, the Great Depression, and loneliness and fear during World War II. But they passed down the most precious gift possible to me. They raised me in a home with peace. It wasn't so much what they *did* as what they *didn't* do—I suffered no abuses as many of my peers did (verbal, sexual, physical, or emotional). And I was loved enough to be made to obey! A generation who had faced the Nazis did not quake when a toddler threw a temper tantrum, nor were they shocked when a youngster deliberately lied. They did not throw their arms up in surrender when a teenager decided to test the boundaries. I was cherished enough to be taught right from wrong, but more importantly, it was modeled in front of me every day. When wrongs were committed by my parents, forgiveness was asked, and restoration made. At any time, someone could have held a grudge, given way to untempered anger, taken revenge, or decided to quit. My parents' commitment to each other and to the principles found in the Word of God—the Ten Commandments and the Golden Rule—held fast. This has allowed my imagination and creativity to run free. The heritage I received from my parents and grandparents has now been passed and is still being passed to my own children, the fourth generation. I have lavished it on them and others. But like my grandfather, if I hadn't received it, I could have chosen to create it from scratch. This is what God had in mind when He had the psalmist write:

> He decreed statutes for Jacob and established the law in Israel,
> which he commanded our forefathers to teach their children,
> So the next generation would know them,
> even the children yet to be born,
> and they in turn would tell their children.
> Then they would put their trust in God
> and would not forget his
> deeds but would keep his commands.
> (Psalm 78:5-7 NIV)

Remember, it all began with a choice. Choices are the hinges on which our heritage swings. We can choose to perpetuate the good handed to us, or reject the good and replace it with bad choices. We can choose to perpetuate the bad, or lay it aside and replace it with good choices. I was sent to this generation as a messenger from a man who was illegitimate, uneducated, and signed his name with an X. This man probably suffered many of the things in life that you have suffered. But he *chose* to create for me a legacy of love and freedom, and I am choosing to create one with my husband, J. Otis. This is my story. We hope you will use it as a springboard and inspiration to keep your family flame burning.

Sources

How to Lead Your Child to Christ

Some things to consider ahead of time:

* Realize that God is more concerned about your child's eternal destiny and happiness than you are. "The Lord is not slack concerning his promise, . . . but is longsuffering to us-ward, not willing that any should perish, but that all should come to repentance" (2 Peter 3:9 KJV).

* Beforehand, pray specifically that God will give you insights and wisdom in dealing with each child on his maturity level.

* Don't use terms like "take Jesus into your heart," "dying and going to hell," or "accepting Christ as your personal Savior." Children are either too literal ("How does Jesus breathe in my heart?"), or the words are too cliché and trite for their understanding.

* Deal with each child alone and don't be in a hurry. Make sure she understands; discuss it until she does. Take your time.

A few cautions:

When drawing children to Himself, Jesus said ALLOW them to come to Him. Only with adults did He use the term

COMPEL. Do not **compel** children. See Mark 10:14, and Luke 14:23. Remember that unless God Himself is speaking through the Holy Spirit to the child, there will be no genuine heart experience of regeneration. Parents, don't get caught up in the idea that Jesus will return the day before you were going to speak to your child about salvation, and that it will be too late. Look at God's character—He **IS** love! He is not dangling your child's soul over hell. Wait on God's timing. Pray, with faith, believing. Be concerned, but don't push.

The plan

Prepare ahead of time and know the Scriptures to use.

God loves you.

Recite John 3:16. Recite it again with your child's name in place of "the world."

You need the Savior.

✳ Deal with sin carefully. Say, "there is one thing that cannot enter heaven—SIN."

✳ Be sure the child knows what sin is. Ask her to name some. (Things common to children—lying, sassing, disobeying, etc.). Sin is DOING or THINKING anything wrong according to God's Word.

✳ Ask, "Have you sinned?"

If the answer is, "No," do NOT continue. Assure him that when he does feel like he has sinned, to come and talk to you again. Some parents may want to have prayer, thanking God "for this young child who is willing to do what is right." Make it easy for him to talk to you again, but do not continue. Do not say, "Oh, yes, you have too sinned!" and then name some. With children, wait for God's conviction.

If the answer is "Yes," continue. He may even give a personal illustration of some sin he has done recently or one that has bothered him.

* Tell him what God says about sin: **We've all sinned.**
"There is none righteous, no, not one" (Rom. 3:10 KJV). "For
all have sinned, and come short of the glory of God"
(Rom. 3:23 KJV). **Because of that sin, we can't get to God,**
"For the wages of sin is death . . . " (Rom. 6:23 KJV); **so He
had to come to us,** ". . . but the gift of God is eternal life
through Jesus Christ our Lord" (Rom. 6:23 KJV).

* Relate God's gift of salvation to receiving Christmas
gifts—we don't earn this gift or pay for it; we just accept it
and are thankful for it.

Make a definite decision.

Explain that Christ must be received if salvation is to be possessed
but, remember, DO NOT FORCE A DECISION. Ask your child to
pray, out loud, in his own words. Give him some things he could
say if he seems unsure. It is best to avoid having the child repeat a
prayer after you. Let him think and make it personal.** Now be
prepared for a blessing! After salvation has occurred, *you* pray for
him out loud. Pronounce a blessing on your child.

God will never leave you.

Show her that she will be able to keep her relationship open
with God through repentance and forgiveness (just like with
her family and friends), and that God will always love her. "I
will never leave thee, nor forsake thee" (Heb. 13:5, KJV).

Teach him his "family" responsibilities:

Show that now that he is a member of God's family, His
child, he has some responsibilities: The Big Five: (1) to pray,
(2) to know more about God (reading the Bible), (3) to love
God's church, (4) to love others (The Golden Rule: "Do unto
others as you would have them do unto you"), and (5) to
give to God's work.

✳✳ If you wish to guide your child through the prayer, here is some suggested language:

Dear God, I know that I am a sinner [have child name specific sins he or she acknowledged earlier, such as lying, stealing, disobeying, etc.]. I know that Jesus died on the cross to pay for all my sins. I ask you to forgive me of my sins. I believe that Jesus died for me and rose from the dead, and I now take Him as my Savior. Thank You for loving me. In Jesus' name. Amen."

Recommended Books

Family Life:

Christenson, Larry, *The Wonderful Way That Babies Are Made*, Bethany House, 1982

Dobson, James, *The New Dare to Discipline*, Tyndale, 1992
  Love Must Be Tough, Word, 1996
  Parenting Isn't For Cowards, Word, 1987
  Preparing For Adolescence, Regal, 1989
  Preparing For Adolescence Family Guide Workbook, Regal, 1989

Elwell, Ellen Banks, *The Christian Mom's Idea Book*, Crossway Books, 1997

Erickson, Donna, *Rainy Day Fun Book*, Augsburg, 1996
  Prime Time Together With Kids, Augsburg, 1989
  More Prime Time Together With Kids, Augsburg, 1992

Gaither, Gloria & Shirley Dobson, *Let's Make A Memory*, Word, 1994
  Let's Hide God's Word, Word, 1994

Hartley, Hermine, *The Family Book of Manners*, Barbour, 1990

Higgs, Liz, *Only Angels Can Wing It, The Rest of Us Have to Practice*, Nelson Word, 1995

Joy, Donald M., *Parents, Kids, & Sexual Integrity*, Word, 1988

Ledbetter, J. Otis & Kurt Bruner, *The Heritage*, Chariot Victor, 1996

Mains, Karen Burton, *Making Sunday Special*, Star Song, 1994

Partow, Cameron & Donna, *Families That Play Together*, Bethany House, 1996

Rainey, Dennis, *One Home At a Time*, Focus on the Family, 1997

Simon, Dr. Mary Manz, *Front Porch Parenting*, Chariot Victor, 1997

Smith, Tim, *Almost Cool*, Moody, 1997
The Relaxed Parent, Northfield, 1996

Weidmann, Jim & Kurt Bruner, *An Introduction to Family Nights*, Chariot Victor, 1997
Basic Christian Beliefs, Chariot Victor, 1997
Christian Character Qualities, Chariot Victor, 1998
Holiday Family Nights, Chariot Victor, 1998
Money Matters Family Nights, Chariot Victor, 1998
Wisdom Life Skills, Chariot Victor, 1998

Winans, Ruth and Linda Lee, *Giving Love a Memory*, Harvest House, 1997

Especially For Mom/Wife:

Baker, Jennifer, *501 Practical Ways to Love Your Husband & Kids*, Concordia House, 1996

Barnes, Emilie, *If Teacups Could Talk*, Harvest House, 1994
Timeless Treasures, Harvest House, 1996

Brestin, Dee, *The Friendships of Women*. Chariot Victor, 1988

Crosby, Harriet, *A Well-Watered Garden*, (A devotional for lady gardeners), Thomas Nelson, 1995

Linda Dillow, *Creative Counterpoint*, Thomas Nelson, 1986

Gibbs, Terri (Editor), *Heartstrings of Laughter and Love*, Word, 1997

Smith, Pam, *Eat Well, Live Well*, Creation House, 1992

Tucker, Ruth, *Seasons of Motherhood, A Garden of Memories*, Chariot Victor, 1996

Wilson, Mimi & Mary Beth Lagerborg, *Table Talk*, Focus on the Family, 1994

Recommended Magazines

Christianity Today (14 issues, P. O. Box 37059, Boone, IA 50037-0059, $24.95)

Country Women (12 issues, P. O. Box 5276, Harlan, Iowa 51593-0794, $16.98)

Focus on the Family (12 issues, P.O. Box 35500, Colorado Springs, Colorado, 80935-3550, free)

Moody (6 issues, P. O. Box 51884, Boulder, CO 80323-1887, $18.95)

New Man (8 issues, P. O. Box 420632, Palm Coast, FL 32142-8874, $21.00)

Single-Parent Family (12 issues, 8605 Explorer Drive, Colorado Springs, C0 80920-1051, Suggested donation, $15.00/yr)

Sports Spectrum (10 issues, P. O. Box 3566, Grand Rapids, MI 49502-0244, $15.97)

Today's Christian Woman (6 issues, P. O. Box 11621, Des Moines, IA 50340-1621, $17.95)

Victoria (12 issues, P. O. Box 7148, Red Oak, IA 51591-2148, $21.97)

Songs to Teach Your Children

Simplest Preschool Songs

Baa Baa Black Sheep	Oats, Peas, Beans and Barley Grow
Bingo	Old MacDonald Had a Farm
Eencey Weencey Spider	Pop Goes the Weasel
Here We Go 'Round the Mulberry Bush	Ring Around the Rosies
The Hokey Pokey	Row, Row, Row Your Boat
If You're Happy and You Know It	Sing a Song of Sixpence
I've Been Working on the Railroad	Three Blind Mice
Mary Had a Little Lamb	Twinkle, Twinkle, Little Star

Be Careful Little Eyes

The B-I-B-L-E

Deep and Wide

Down in My Heart

Fishers of Men

God Is So Good

Hallelu, Praise Ye the Lord

He's Got the Whole World in His Hands

I Am a Promise

If You're Saved and You Know It

I'm in the Lord's Army

Jesus Loves Me

Jesus Loves the Little Children

Little David Played on His Harp

Oh, How I Love Jesus

Only a Boy Named David

This Little Light of Mine

Wide As the Ocean

Early School Years

The Ants Go Marching

Clementine

Down by the Riverside

Frere Jacques

He's Got the Whole World in His Hand

Home on the Range

If I Had a Hammer

London Bridge Is Falling Down

Michael, Row the Boat Ashore

Mister Frog Went a Courtin'

Oh Susanna

On Top of Spaghetti

Rise and Shine

She'll Be Comin' Round the Mountain

Skip, Skip, Skip to My Lou

Take Me Out to the Ball Game

This Land Is Your Land

Yankee Doodle

All Day, All Night

Alleluia

Arky, Arky

Assurance March (Can We Know)

Boys and Girls for Jesus

Do Lord

Give Me Oil in My Lamp

Go Tell It on the Mountain

He's Been Working on Me

His Banner Over Me Is Love

Into My Heart

I've Got Peace Like a River

I Wanna Be Just Like the Lord

I Will Sing of the Mercies

Jesus Loves Even Me

Joshua Fit the Battle of Jericho

Kum Ba Yah

Only a Boy Named David

Rejoice in the Lord Always

Thank You, Lord

This Is the Day

There Is Power in the Name of Jesus

The Heritage Builders Concept

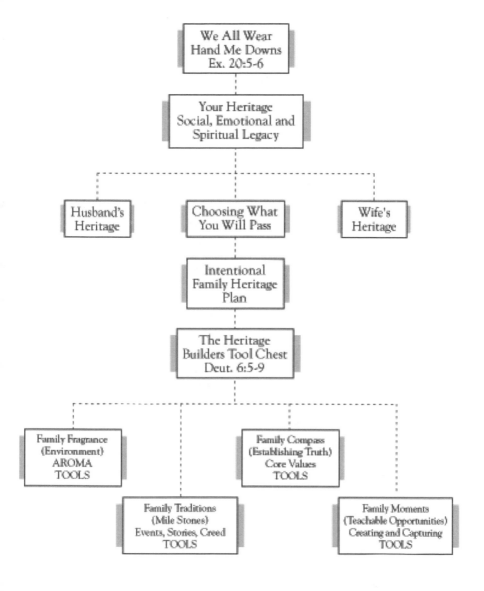

Psalm 78: 1 - 8

Endnotes

Introduction
1   Ledbetter, J. Otis and Kurt Bruner, *Your Heritage.* Colorado Springs: Chariot Victor, 1996, pp. 101-102.

Chapter One
1   McGervey, John D. and Bill Sones, "How Sensitive Are You?" *Reader's Digest,* May, 1996, Buffalo, NY, p. 91.
2   Rader, Dotson, "A Chance To Go the Distance," *Parade* Magazine, July 6, 1997, p. 4-5.
3   Robert Bezell and Dr. Craig Warren, *NBC Nightly News,* May 13, 1996, "The Sense of Smell."
4   Lewis, C.S., *The Four Loves,* Harcourt Brace Jovanonich, 1960, p. 68.

Chapter Two
1   *Noah Webster's First Edition of an American Dictionary of the English Language,* 1828, permission to reprint granted by G&C Merriam Company (Foundation for American Christian Education, San Francisco, 1967).
2   Mattox, William R. Jr., *Citizen* Magazine, Focus on the Family, November 1997, pp. 19 & 21.
3   Ibid., p. 19.
4   *Marketing Management, Shaping the Profession of Marketing,* Winter, 1994, Vol. 3, No. 3.
5   Ledbetter, J. Otis & Kurt Bruner, *Your Heritage,* Chariot Victor, 1996, p. 249.

Chapter Three
1   *Family Circle* Magazine, 7-18-95, p. 52.
2   *Noah Webster's First Edition of an American Dictionary of the English Language,* 1828, permission to reprint granted by G&C Merriam Company, (Foundation for American Christian Education, San Francisco, 1967).
3   Ledbetter/Bruner, *Your Heritage,* Chariot Victor, 1996, p 110.

Chapter Four
1   *Noah Webster's First Edition of an American Dictionary of the English Language,* 1828, permission to reprint granted by G&C Merriam Company, (Foundation for American Christian Education, San Francisco, 1967).
2   John Rosemond, "Parenting," *The Fresno Bee,* July 27, 1997, E4. Used by permission.

Chapter Five
1   *Noah Webster's First Edition of an American Dictionary of the English Language,* 1828, permission to reprint granted by G&C Merriam Company, (Foundation of American Christian Education, San Francisco, 1967).
2   C.S. Lewis, *The Screwtape Letters,* MacMillan, 1982, p 9.
3   Jane Canfield, Quote/Unquote comp. by Lloyd Cory, Chariot Victor, 1977, p 144.

Chapter Six
1   *Noah Webster's First Edition of an American Dictionary of the Enlish Language,* 1828, permission to reprint granted by G&C Merriam Company, (Foundation for American Christian Education, San Francisco, 1967).
2   J. Otis Ledbetter and Kurt Bruner, *Your Heritage,* Chariot Victor, 1996, p 108.